STOCK MARKET
STRATEGIES THAT WORK

STOCK MARKET STRATEGIES THAT WORK

Jacob Bernstein

Elliott Bernstein

McGraw-Hill
New York   Chicago   San Francisco
Lisbon   London   Madrid   Mexico City   Milan
New Delhi   San Juan   Seoul   Singapore
Sydney   Toronto

Library of Congress Cataloging-in-Publication Data

Bernstein, Jacob.
    Stock market strategies that work / by Jacob & Elliott Bernstein.
       p. cm.
    ISBN: 0-07-138194-5
    1. Stocks.   2. Speculation.   I. Bernstein, E. R. (Elliott L.)   II. Title.

    HG4661.B463 2002
    332.63'22—dc21

                                    2001045280

McGraw-Hill

A Division of The McGraw·Hill Companies

1 2 3 4 5 6 7 8 9 0 DOC/DOC 0 7 6 5 4 3 2 1

0-07-138194-5

The sponsoring editor for this book was Stephen Isaacs, the editing supervisor was Ruth W. Mannino, and the production supervisor was Clare Stanley. It was set in Times by Patricia Wallenburg.

Printed and bound by R. R. Donnelley and Sons Company.

This publication is designed to provide accurate and authoritative information in regard to the subject matter covered. It is sold with the understanding that neither the author nor the publisher is engaged in rendering legal, accounting, or other professional service. If legal advice or other expert assistance is required, the services of a competent professional person should be sought.

> *—From a Declaration of Principles jointly adopted*
> *by a Committee of the American Bar*
> *Association and a Committee of Publishers*

McGraw-Hill books are available at special quantity discounts to use as premiums and sales promotions, or for use in corporate training programs. For more information, please write to the Director of Special Sales, Professional Publishing, McGraw-Hill, Two Penn Plaza, New York, NY 10121-2298. Or contact your local bookstore.

 This book is printed on recycled, acid-free paper containing a minimum of 50% recycled de-inked fiber.

CONTENTS

LIST OF ILLUSTRATIONS   ix

PREFACE   xiii

ACKNOWLEDGMENTS   xv

1   BEGINNINGS   1

The Big Lie   2
The Experts Failed   3
Risk Capital: The Bottom Line   4
Can You Make Money in the Market without a Computer?   9
Summary   9

2   PLAYING THE GAME   11

    A Share of What?   11
    How Charts Help You Play the Game for Big Money   13
    Keeping Things Simple and Effective   18
    Trading on Margin   20
    Buy Low and Sell High or Buy High and Sell Higher?
    Two Ways to Play the Game   22
    Summary   24

3   THE DOS AND DON'TS OF
    PICKING WINNING STOCKS   27

    A Few Basic Keys That Will Help You Pick Winning Stocks   27
    What's a Tech Stock?   33
    What's a Medical Stock?   34
    What's an IPO?   34
    Summary   36

4   PICKING A STOCKBROKER   37

    If You're Ready to Trade   38
    Why Are Commission Costs So Important?   39
    Do You Need All the Free Stuff?   39
    What's the Difference?   39
    Summary   41

5   TRADING THE CHEAPIES   43

    Volume   44
    Who Are They?   45
    Number of Outstanding Shares   46
    Institutional Ownership: Trading with the Gorillas   47
    Insider Activity   48
    Low-Priced Stocks with High Short Interest   48
    Sex Appeal   49
    How to Buy and Sell Stocks Under $10   50
    Penny Stocks   51
    Too Many Choices for One Investor!   52
    Low-Priced Mutual Funds   52
    Summary   53

6   THE TECHNICAL APPROACH TO
     STOCK MARKET STRATEGIES   55

     Timing Indicators, Systems, and Methods   55
     Types of Timing Indicators   57
     An Examination of Basic Timing Indicators   60
     Elements of an Effective Stock Trading System   82
     Support and Resistance Concepts   83
     The Value of Day Trading with Support and Resistance   85
     Summary   87

7   DOLLAR COST AVERAGING   89

     About DCA   90
     How Dollar Cost Averaging Works   90
     Summary   91

8   SUPPORT AND RESISTANCE: THE MAC   93

     Determining Support and Resistance   95
     The Moving Average Channel   95
     How Support and Resistance Develop   97
     Five Successive Bars   107
     Exiting Positions, Right or Wrong   107
     Channel Surfing   113
     A Few Precautions and Suggestions   113
     Summary   119

9   TWO REAL-TIME EXAMPLES   121

     Doing My Homework   122
     Why Fuel Cell?   123
     Timing the Trade   124
     Safety First   125
     Another Example   126
     Summary   128

10   IMPLEMENTING MARKET STRATEGIES   129

     Using MOMMA   129
     Dollar Cost Averaging with Mutual Fund Investments   135
     A Comparison of Strategies   137
     Wrap Up   140
     Summary   140

11 THE IMPORTANCE OF DISCIPLINE
Maximizing Profits, Minimizing Losses, Following the Rules   141

Trading Discipline: A Working Definition   142
The Three Levels of Investing Discipline   144
Closing Out Losers   145
A Closer Look at Fear   147
Overcoming the Fear of Investing   149
A Few Closing Thoughts about Discipline   149
Conclusion   150
Summary   151

12 COMPUTERIZED TRADING SYSTEMS   153

Buy into the Myth   154
Defining the Reality   155
Let the Buyer Beware!   155
Why Test a Trading System?   156
Summary   167

GLOSSARY OF TRADING TERMS   173

INDEX   181

LIST OF
ILLUSTRATIONS

Figure 2-1. A daily price chart.   14

Figure 2-2. A weekly price chart.   15

Figure 2-3. A monthly price chart.   16

Figure 2-4. An intraday ten-minute price chart.   17

Figure 6-1. Daily Affymetrix (AFFX) chart with
five different MAs (6, 12, 18, 56, and 120).   62

Figure 6-2. Daily Affymetrix (AFFX) chart with MACD
buy-and-sell signals (MACD values = 0.218, 0.108, and 0.199).   64

Figure 6-3. Daily AT&T chart with stochastic signals
(stochastic 9- period, RSI 3-period).   66

Figure 6-4. Daily Priceline.com chart with parabolic indicator
    (step factor 0.02).   69

Figure 6-5. ADX signals on a daily Brocade Communications chart.   71

Figure 6-6. Daily IBM chart with 28-period momentum.
    (When momentum is above zero, trend is bullish;
    when below, trend is bearish.)   73

Figure 6-7. Accumulation and distribution on a daily
    chart of RealNetworks, Inc. (RNWK).   75

Figure 6-8. Accumulation and distribution on a daily
    chart of Cisco Systems (CSCO).   77

Figure 6-9. Williams and Waters' accumulation/distribution
    (A/D) oscillator an a daily Amazon.com (AMZN) chart.   79

Figure 6-10. Daily chart of Amazon.com with ADD and signals.   80

Figure 6-11. Weekly chart of Amazon.com with ADD and signals.   81

Figure 6-12. Support on daily Corr Therapeutics chart.   84

Figure 6-13. Resistance in daily Agilent Technologies (A) chart.   86

Figure 8-1. Daily MAC (Citrix Systems).   96

Figure 8-2. Daily MAC (IBM).   98

Figure 8-3. Daily MAC (JNPR).   99

Figure 8-4. MAC buy and sell signals (BRCM).   100

Figure 8-5. MAC buy and sell signals (BRCD).   101

Figure 8-6. MAC buy and sell signals (SCP).   102

Figure 8-7. MAC buy and sell signals (ADM).   103

Figure 8-8. MAC buy and sell signals (BA).   104

Figure 8-9. MAC buy and sell signals (MFST).   105

Figure 8-10. MAC buy and sell signals (Dow Jones).   106

Figure 8-11. MAC five bar signals (GILD).   108

Figure 8-12. MAC five bar signals (QQQ).   109

Figure 8-13. MAC five bar signals (EBAY).   110

Figure 8-14. MAC five bar signals (CMGI).   111

Figure 8-15. MAC five bar signals (CORR).   112

Figure 8-16. MAC channel surfing (MOT).   114

Figure 8-17. MAC channel surfing (AOL).   115

Figure 8-18. MAC channel surfing (CORR).   116

Figure 8-19. MAC channel surfing (SFA).   117

Figure 8-20. MAC channel surfing (AMAT).   118

Figure 9-1. Three-month daily chart of FCEL.   127

Figure 10-1. CHINA with MOM/MA plotted below.   131

Figure 10-2. Three-month daily chart of CHINA with MOM/MA plotted below; a closer look.   132

Figure 10-3. RYOIX with DCA points based on MOM/MA signals.   138

Figure 12-1. The 3-MA system in Intel, 1998–2001.   159

Figure 12-2. The 3-MA system in Intel, 1990–2001.   160

Figure 12-3. The 3-MA system in Intel, 1980–2001.   161

Figure 12-4. The 3-MA system in Intel, 1978–2001.   162

Figure 12-5. A 3-MA system, 1990–2001.   163

Figure 12-6. A 3-MA system, 1980–2001.   164

Figure 12-7. A 3-MA system, 1970–2001.   168

Figure 12-8. A 3-MA system with different inputs, 1970–2001.   169

Figure 12-9. The 3-MA system in Eli Lilly, 1999–2001.   170

Figure 12-10. The 3-MA system in Eli Lilly, 1990–2001.   171

PREFACE

The investment jungle is a dangerous place in which only the fittest survive and prosper. The average investor who attempts to profit without the assistance of a professional, competent adviser or money manager is, all too often, grist for the mill. Large investment machines feed, without mercy, on the small trader who, all too readily, ventures into the wilderness, defenseless and without a clue.

This book will help new investors find a place of refuge and knowledge where they can acquire the skills necessary for survival and profit in the brutal world of investing. Armed with the information, tools, skills, knowledge, techniques, and methods provided in this book, the new or small investor can compete successfully with the lions, often beating them at their own game.

Stock Market Strategies That Work offers all investors, whether experienced or new to the markets, powerful tools for success, all presented in a down-to-earth, often humorous, but always clear and concise fashion.

In 1998 the authors of this book, realizing the plight of new investors and traders, initiated the 2chimps.com Web site. The premises upon which 2chimps.com and this book are based are as follow:

- The stock market is risky and dangerous unless you have and use effective trading tools.

- The stock market jungle is likely to gobble up small investors and other defenseless creatures unless they are able to protect themselves with solid skills and tools.

- Large beasts of prey in the investment jungle (lions, tigers, leopards, and the like) often eat the smaller beasts such as monkeys.

- Most of us are market monkeys; we are often victims rather than victors.

- Market monkeys often fall prey to herd mentality, following one another off the cliff into the abyss of losses.

- Our goal as market chimps is to overcome the numerous obstacles that prevent us from being successful in stocks.

Your two chief market chimps, Elliott and Jacob, with their staff of skilled simian stock seers, make it look easy. Why? Because it is easy!

We cut through the mounds of pretentious rhetoric and obligatory financial trash talk, leaving behind the clear and coherent facts.

During the course of this book we may, from time to time, use analogies to the investment jungle. Do not take offense. These terms and analogies are only intended to be comic relief in order to deal lightly with a topic that is all too often presented in a dull or boring fashion.

Jacob and Elliott Bernstein
Winnetka, Illinois
May 2001

ACKNOWLEDGMENTS

The authors wish to express their thanks to the following individuals and/or organizations who have each, in their own special way, contributed greatly to the final product.

- Marilyn Kinney for helping us remain motivated, organized, and on task.
- Nan Martin Barnum for her skills in proofreading, editing, and the physical layout of the original manuscript.
- The Bernstein family and friends for their encouragement in helping us bring together the diverse ideas and methods contained in this book.
- The good people at Commodity Quote Graphics (CQG) and TradeStation Technologies for permission to use their charts and technical market indicators.

- The editing staff at McGraw-Hill, both in New York and in Chicago.
- And finally, Mr. Stephen Isaacs, Acquisitions Editor at McGraw-Hill, who believed strongly enough in our abilities to give us this wonderful opportunity.

STOCK MARKET
STRATEGIES THAT WORK

CHAPTER

1

BEGINNINGS

" 'Tis always morning somewhere in the world."
Richard Henry Horne

Let's begin by understanding a few important concepts. This chapter will introduce you to several of the essential ideas. We will then build on the basics to give you the tools and skills you need to invest profitably. But before we do that, let's establish a few facts that are vital to your effective use of the lessons you will learn in this book. Some of you may not agree with our conclusions. In fact, some of you may take offense at what we say. If this is the case, then please accept our apologies in advance. Remember that this book approaches the topic of making money in stocks from the practical point of view.

We aren't going to bore you with scholarly arguments or economic theory. We're simply going to tell things to you the way we see them (which is the way we think things really are). In so doing we will undoubtedly make a few enemies and alienate a number of people within the stock market community. But we do not do so intentionally. We merely believe that every industry has its vested interests and groups of individuals or organizations that want to keep information from being disseminated to the general public. In stating things as we see them, we will open the doors to success for those who have the motivation and persistence to cross the threshold of knowledge.

Those within the investment community who feel that new players in the game may threaten their potential income are likely to object vehemently to what we will say and teach in this book. Be forewarned that the traditional investment community does not commonly accept some of the methods and approaches we teach in this book. So let's not waste another moment. Let's begin alienating people immediately!

THE BIG LIE

There are those who believe that in order to be successful in the stock market you need to gather as much information as possible about a given company. They believe that you need to know a company's earnings, products, quality of management, market share, growth prospects, finances, and accounting procedures. They further believe that any inside information you can get will also be helpful. This type of fundamental information can be useful; however, there is no guarantee that it will work any better than the purely technical approach you will learn in this book.

If you tell your friends or family that you don't care about what a company does, or worse, that you have no idea what they do but you're buying their stock regardless, then you will surely be considered either a fool or reckless. After all, it is commonly accepted wisdom that you need to know what a company does in order to make money by investing in or trading in its stock.

That's the first big lie about investing. While such information *can* make you money in the long run, there are no certainties. The history of the stock market is replete with examples of such information being rendered utterly useless by intervening or unexpected events. The dot-com debacle of the early 2000s is a classic example of how the best analysts and brokerage houses in the world miscalculated, misunderstood, and misadvised their clients about the growth prospects of an industry group that was touted as "the wave of the future."

THE EXPERTS FAILED

Market analysts studied the business prospects for Internet firms and technology firms. They projected earnings five years into the future. They projected the growth of the Internet and the supposedly massive market for Internet advertising. And this led them to project the prices of certain stocks to highly inflated and totally unreasonable levels. Gullible investors bought the hype and poured billions of dollars into worthless stocks, buying them at very high prices only to see these stocks drop to under $10 per share over the next twelve to sixteen months.

The dot-com disaster is merely one example of how investors have been sold a bill of goods. They have been led to believe that solid fundamental research produces profits. The truth is that fundamental research is no better than the individual who does the research, and it is no better than the independence of the individual who does the research. Those with a vested interest will see what they want to see and not what they need to see. In truth, there are only a few fundamental analysts who are truly skilled at their craft. We believe that you can be more successful using the technical approaches in this book than you can by following fundamental analysis.

No doubt these strong words will create some friction. But we believe that the facts bear out our opinions. If fundamentals were truly the best path to profits, then experienced money managers would rarely experience periods of decline in their holdings. Their fundamentals would tell them ahead of time when stock trends were going to reverse, and they would take the necessary action. If you spend a few minutes looking at the price fluctuations of even the best-managed mutual funds, you'll see large swings over time. If the fundamentals were all-knowing, then the price swings would not be as severe. In fact, they might not exist at all. Money managers with great skill would have such effective strategies that their mutual fund share price would be on a steady upswing with only minor declines.

We respectfully suggest that the average individual without a degree in finance or economics can do just as well or even better than the professional *if* he or she uses the right technical tools combined with a systematic approach to risk management and self-discipline. So forget about the books that teach you how to analyze a stock based on the fundamentals. We aim to teach you things that can work just as well or better and that require much less effort, no education in finance, and no intense studies of industries or industry groups.

To put things simply, this book will give you the tools, understanding, methods, and procedures you need to compete effectively in the stock market. We believe that you can acquire these tools within a reasonable amount of time and with a reasonable amount of effort. And, if you practice them, you'll quickly be on your way to successful investing and trading.

RISK CAPITAL: THE BOTTOM LINE

The goal of all trading or investing is to make money. Yes, there are some secondary gains such as the thrill of victory and the challenge of the game. But make no mistake about it: Profit is the one and only goal on which you must focus your energies. But in order to arrive at your goal, there are various vehicles, tools, and rules that must be understood. We will teach these to you in the chapters that follow.

Once you have acquired the knowledge this book will impart, you will need to have some risk capital with which to invest or trade. Before discussing how much money you will need as your starting point, let's define two terms that we've already used a number of times and which should have been defined earlier. When we talk about *investing*, we are referring to a longer-term approach to making money the capitalist way. We use money to make money, but it takes more than a few days or a few weeks.

Although there is no hard and fast definition as to what constitutes an *investment* as opposed to a *trade*, we will define it specifically for the purposes of this book. We like to think of an *investment* as any use of money that is expected to require a holding period of three months or longer. By exclusion then, a *trade* is the use of money over a period of time up to three months in length but longer than one day in length. *Trading* is a relatively short-term proposition whereas *investing* is longer term. A day trade, on the other hand, is exactly what its name implies. A *day trade* is the use of money in an effort to profit within the time frame of one day.

Over the years, things have changed markedly in the stock market. Since the mid-1980s, the markets have been moving up and down rapidly. Prices have been highly volatile. While it may once have taken six months for the price of a stock to move from $30 to $40, such moves today can occur in a matter of several days and, on occasion, in a single day! This situation has, by necessity, created many opportunities over short periods of time. Individuals who once considered themselves investors have now become traders. And some have even become day traders in order to capitalize on the often-large intraday price swings in many stocks.

In practice, there are only a few considerations in determining whether one wants to be a trader or an investor. There are tax advantages to investing as opposed to trading. But if the amount of money you can make as a trader is larger and faster than what you can make as an investor, then the larger tax may be worth paying.

In addition, trading often requires more attention and commitment than does investing. If you have very limited time to give to this venture (or adventure, as the case may be), then you may want to use the techniques in this book for picking investments rather than trades. But to us it matters little as long as you have familiarized yourself with the risks and rewards.

Let's begin by considering the amount of risk capital you will need in order to play the trading or investing game. The minimum balance with which you can open an account with even the deepest discount brokers is $500.[1] So, technically, you cannot begin trading with only a "hundred bucks." That is not to say that people don't start trading with only $500. Most online brokers advertise that you can begin trading with as little as that. Truthfully, there is no catch; they will not penalize you for having a small account. But when you start trading with a small amount of cash, you penalize yourself because you limit your opportunities for success.

As an example, consider the fact that if you make a trade and lose $200 of your $500, you have also limited how much money you have available for your next trade. If you lose another $200 the next time then you might as well quit, since your chances of success are slim. The simple fact is that you need enough money to allow for a number of successive losses in your trading. You are far better off waiting a year to accumulate a good starting amount of capital than you are in starting with only a few hundred dollars. The less you start with, the worse your odds of success.

What Can You Do with $500?

If you must begin investing in stocks with $500, there are a few ways to improve your chances of success. The best way is to put your money into *mutual funds*. What we're essentially telling you here is that if you only have $500, you ought to put it into a conservative investment that will be handled by professional traders in a large pool of money. Professionally managed mutual funds can be bought and sold in a similar fashion to stocks. When you buy a mutual fund, you are essentially giving your money to the fund manager who invests it in a number of stocks he or she believes will be profitable. The benefits such funds offer the investor with limited cash are exposure to a wider number of stocks as well as the access to the prudence and skill of a professional investor.

Although mutual funds can be traded to some degree, we do not suggest you try to do this. Such funds are meant for long-term investment, and the true rewards of investing in mutual funds are often seen only after several years to a decade. If you want to start investing a little more proactively, save up your cash until you have a bit more than $500. Actually, $1000 would be a much better starting amount. In fact, we would suggest this as the bare minimum amount.

---

[1] This will likely change over time.

What Can You Do with $1000?

Starting with $1000 is a little more promising. Doing this, you are able to buy 100 shares of a $9 or $10 stock. However, your portfolio will still be extremely unbalanced if you choose to invest this way. If your one bet turns out wrong, you end up losing everything. Even with $1000, investing in mutual funds is a wise move.

Another strategy for investing with $1000 is to buy *odd lots*. This basically means that you will be buying less than 100 shares of a given stock. Say you want to buy AT&T at the price of $22 per share. You could potentially buy as many as forty-five shares of this stock. However, this would leave you with no money to buy other stocks. You like AT&T, but you are not 100 percent sure its stock will rise in value. Instead, you buy ten shares, which costs you $220. Instead of AT&T comprising 100 percent of your portfolio, it now comprises 20 percent. This is still a significant position; however, it is considerably smaller than buying forty-five shares. Now you can research other stocks that appeal to you (something you will be learning how to do very soon) and buy small numbers of shares as well.

Buying and selling odd lots has become easier since the advent of Internet trading. However, it is still hard to succeed by investing this way because fo the cost of commissions. We'll cover this more in depth later, but to give you a general idea, commissions are the fees you pay for trading. Every time you buy or sell a stock, you must pay your broker a set fee of somewhere between $5 and $50. In order to make money by trading odd lots, you have to be able to make more money than the commission for both buying and selling. This is not as easy as it may sound.

What's a Reasonable Starting Amount?

We recommend starting with at least $3000. A little less is still acceptable. A little or a lot more is better. Remember that the more money you start with, the greater your chances of making money in the market. Don't go overboard and make a snap decision to invest your entire nest egg. The reason we suggest $3000 is because it will give you flexibility and, although it is a substantial amount of money, you will most likely not be permanently harmed by its loss. If you feel that losing $3000 would do this kind of damage, you might want to wait until you have become more financially secure before you invest.

We suggest the $3000 as a starting sum for several other reasons. First of all, this sum generally allows you to trade without worrying about taking small losses in the beginning. When trading with only $500, you have to watch every penny. Losing $50 means losing 10 percent of your account! However, with $3000, commissions of $20 per trade (an average price) and small losses of even $100 or $200 are still bearable and will not put you out of the game right away.

With $3000, you will be able to make decisions about trades based on your own analysis, rather than based on how much the trade has cost you. Some of your strategies may leave room for a stock to fall in price before it begins to rise. Having enough money in your account gives you the cushioning you need to employ such trading methods. This sum also allows you to trade what you want. You can purchase 100 shares of a $30 stock to 1000 shares of a $3 stock, and everything in between.

Finally, having any amount of money over $2000 in your account allows you to trade on 50 percent *margin* with many brokers. This is just a fancy way of saying that you only have to supply half the money for any stock. If you have $2000 in your account, you have access to up to $4000 to buy stocks. However, brokerage firms will charge you interest for using margin. This is because it is not free money; you are actually borrowing cash from the broker every time you make a margin trade. We will discuss the benefits and drawbacks of margin later. But keep it in mind as an added benefit when you open your account with a larger sum of money.

Can You Believe What You See on the Internet and on TV?

When Chimp Jacob and I began to discuss this topic, we were not of the same opinion. He answered no and I answered sometimes. This is not a surprise; Chimp Jacob is older and less impressionable than I am, and therefore he's more of a skeptic. But I suggested to him that not everything on the television is completely false, and we started to work on a method for you to determine exactly what you should and should not listen to when reading or hearing about the stock market.

Here is what we came up with; *believe only the facts, not the opinions.* It is ridiculous to ask you to unplug your computer, turn off your television, and stop reading the newspaper. But always remember to view these sources of information with a very discerning eye. An industry analyst or company manager who sounds like he or she knows the inside scoop might have ulterior motives. In fact, these people are sometimes the *worst* ones to use as your source of information.

What Are Opinions?

An *opinion* is anything a person says which he or she cannot guarantee will come true. In other words, opinions are very similar to predictions. When you see the CEO of an Internet company on CNBC saying that she sees 500 percent growth in revenues in the next year, this is a prediction as well as an opinion. There are also other disguises for opinions; these are qualitative judgments.

Rather than being based on facts and numbers, *qualitative judgments* are based on the way an individual or group feels about a situation. You hear an industry analyst for gold say that the market for gold looks extremely strong and it should continue to be this way for some time. The first part of this statement, "Gold looks extremely strong," is qualitative *until* you see the numbers that prove its strength. The second part is also qualitative; it is an opinion as well as a prediction.

Who has an opinion? Well, to slightly modify an old aphorism, opinions are like mouths; everybody has one. From newscasters like CNBC's Maria Barteromo to Allen Greenspan, whose opinion many people revere as fact, opinions and mouths pervade our world. Although you should recognize when a person is stating an opinion as opposed to a fact. Certain people's opinions are more dangerous than others.

Beware of stock analysts, company officers like CEOs and CFOs, newsletter writers (present company included), industry spokespeople, government officials, and politicians (who would have guessed?). Why these people? Because many of us have a vested interest in certain stocks. The CEO is responsible for much of the success or failure of his or her company, and therefore is likely to say little to harm public interest in its stock.

In one memorable example, in early December 2000, the CEO and president of Cisco Systems, John Chambers, was "fiercely positive about Cisco's future."[2] Just a few months later, Chambers announced that Cisco would lay off 17 percent of its workforce. Cisco declined from $45 to $11.04 less than a year later.

Industry analysts, newsletter writers, politicians, and others often have connections to the stocks they recommend. Although these links may not be quite as direct and clear as the link of the CEO, they are still present and should be enough to deter you from acting on their opinions.

What Are Facts?

Opinions turn out to be a very large portion of what you read and hear through media. But this does not mean that they are all you can read or hear. You can still find facts. These are data, such as sales statistics, company reports, government reports, earnings announcements, and so on. You can compare this data to previous reports to decide for yourself how a situation looks. You don't always have to find this information yourself; it's fine if a reporter or company spokesperson gives it to you. But beware of spin. Sometimes, not all the data or facts are revealed. In this way, the same people who are giving you facts are creating a façade. Don't be fooled by a clever mixture of the facts they wish you to hear and the opinions they want you to believe. Make your own decisions!

[2] Cathleen Moore, Infoworld.com, *Cisco CEO Optimistic about Future*, Tuesday, December 5, 2000.

CAN YOU MAKE MONEY IN THE MARKET WITHOUT A COMPUTER?

Of course you can make money without a computer. People have been making money trading stocks as well as other investments for hundreds of years without using computers. To assume that there is no way to make money in the market without a computer is wrong. Your goals as an investor or trader may determine decide whether you need to use a computer or not. Trading without a computer may very well be the best. But you can't decide until you know where you are in terms of your needs and abilities as a trader. And this book will help you with that decision.

In the case of long-term investing in stocks, not using a computer can actually be an advantage. Instead of spending valuable time every day checking your stocks to see if you are making or losing money, you maintain a healthy distance from your investments. As a result you are less likely to make decisions based on your emotions. Therefore you will be less tempted to sell after only a few months, when, in fact, you should be holding your investments for as long as a few years.

Finally, if you use an online broker and a computer for placing your orders, your commission costs and fees will be considerably lower than if you use an offline broker with whom you place orders by telephone. All too often investors and traders who use electronic order entry are encouraged to trade more frequently due to the lower commission costs. With a traditional broker, the higher cost of trading helps you maintain your goal as long-term investor, rather than encouraging you to be a short-term trader or a day trader.

Now that we've taken care of a few "nuts and bolts" issues as well as some basic understanding and a few definitions, let's move on to some specifics about how to play this game. We will review many of the essentials as we go along. However, if there is a term you do not understand and if a working definition is not given in the text or glossary at the end of the book, please consult any basic book about the stock market for a definition before you continue reading.

SUMMARY

Investing can be an overwhelming and bewildering prospect to the newcomer. In this chapter, we explain the foundations on which we build our market strategies:

- *Checking company reports, earnings, and other figures is not important when using a technical approach to investing!* You *do not* need to know economics in order to make your investments.

- *Don't let people tell you what to do.* With any approach, it is extremely important that you make your own decisions. Whether you decide to use our investment methods or not, make sure you have your own reasons for buying and selling stocks. Listening to CEOs, stock analysts, and the like, will not help you profit.

We also dispel a few common trading myths:

- *You can start with only a few hundred dollars.* The minimum most brokerage firms require when starting a new account is $500. But much of your success or failure depends on how much money you decide to invest. Starting with $500 leaves you little room for success. Investing in mutual funds may be your best bet with such a small amount of capital. $1000 may be better, but we recommend starting with at least $3000, so that you can handle trading costs as well as a series of successive losses.

- *You can't be successful in today's market without a computer.* This is completely bogus. Although computers are often helpful for day traders and short-term traders, they may actually hurt your long-term investment strategy. It's all right to use a computer if it's more convenient for you, but don't be tempted to check your portfolio every few hours. Such easy access to account balances and other information can make you take actions that are harmful to your investment strategy.

C   H   A   P   T   E   R

PLAYING
THE GAME

"Life's too short for chess."

Henry James Byron

Let's begin at the beginning. For readers who are well versed in the basics, there may be some redundancy in what follows. For this we apologize in advance. We will try to keep our definitions brief and to the point.

A SHARE OF WHAT?

Stocks are traded in shares. Although most people have some idea of what a share is, here are a few basics for those who may be somewhat unclear as to what you are buying or selling when you trade in shares. When you buy or sell a company's stock, you buy it in amounts or units called *shares*.

A share is a part ownership in the company. The price of a share is quoted in dollars (or yen, or Swiss francs, etc.) per share. So, if I hypothetically wanted to buy one share of a $20 stock, I would have to spend $20.

But shares are almost never bought in such small amounts. A *lot*, which is 100 shares of a stock, is the normal minimum amount of shares to buy. An *odd lot*, which is discussed in Chapter 1, is any amount of shares less than 100. If I want to buy 100 shares of the aforementioned $20 stock, I would have to spend $2000.

To calculate how much money you will spend to buy a certain number of shares, use this simple equation:

(Price per share) × (number of shares) = total cost in dollars

Mathematically, the above example looks like this:

($20 per share) × (100 shares) = $2000

All this information is helpful for figuring out how many shares you are going to buy. But you might not want to buy them until you know exactly what they are. Sometimes, the management of a company decides that it would be more profitable for the company if the public were to own parts of it rather than having just a few people own the whole thing. When they make this decision and sell shares in their company to whomever wishes to buy them, the company is said to be *going public*. If your shares increase in value, you make money.

Every time you buy a share, you are buying a piece of ownership in a company. At different times, people will want different amounts of these shares. For example, if the company begins to make large amounts of money, this may cause people to want more shares of the company. The supply of these shares being sold by owners, combined with the demand that buyers have for these shares determines the value, or price, of each share.

Not all shares are equal. Each company decides on its own how much stock to offer to the public. If a company decides to offer only 1000 shares of stock to the public, each one of those shares should theoretically be worth a very large amount, assuming that the company has monetary value and that people want to own parts of that company.

When companies go public, they usually offer millions of shares. The price of shares can be affected by the number of shares issued, because of the laws of supply and demand. Sometimes, a company that is already public decides to issue new stock in order to raise capital (each share sold gives the company additional money). When this happens, the price of the stock should go down, because now there are more shares. Unless demand for the shares goes up, the price will decline.

HOW CHARTS HELP YOU PLAY THE GAME FOR BIG MONEY

If I wanted to get in my car and drive with no particular purpose or destination in mind whatsoever, I could do that without a problem. A similar approach to the stock market, however, can be an expensive proposition. Say you're going to take a long trip in your car. Perhaps your destination is somewhere you've never been before. You don't just get in and go; you bring along a set of directions or a road map. In the stock market, price charts are a lot like road maps. Charts tell you where stocks have been, and with the right tools, they can help you figure out where a stock is going.

What are *price charts*? These are graphs on which the historical prices of a stock are plotted. Stock charts show different periods of time, and can be plotted in different ways. Some common forms of price charts are daily charts, which show a price bar for every day (Figure 2-1); weekly charts (Figure 2-2); monthly charts (Figure 2-3); and intra-day charts (Figure 2-4), which show the movement of a stock price within the span of one day (these charts often use three- or five-minute bars).

What Can Charts Do for You?

Having charts might make you seem smart, and if you stare at them hard enough you might be able to find animal shapes. But how can they actually *help* you? In even their most basic form, charts can help you find historical highs and lows for stocks. Because of the visual nature of the stock chart, it's easy to glance at one and know right away if the price has risen or fallen recently (or at any point in the stock's history).

You can also determine if a stock has been rising or falling quickly relative to how it normally moves. If a stock only trades within a $5 range for a long period of time, and then jumps $10 in one day, you will notice this very easily on a chart.

It is also easy to compare stocks to each other using charts. If you wish to see how a stock has performed relative to a larger index like the Nasdaq or the Dow Jones Industrial Average (DJIA), you can easily plot a chart, which compares the two symbols in percent movement. This is especially useful if you want to determine which of two stocks in a particular sector has performed better in the past or present.

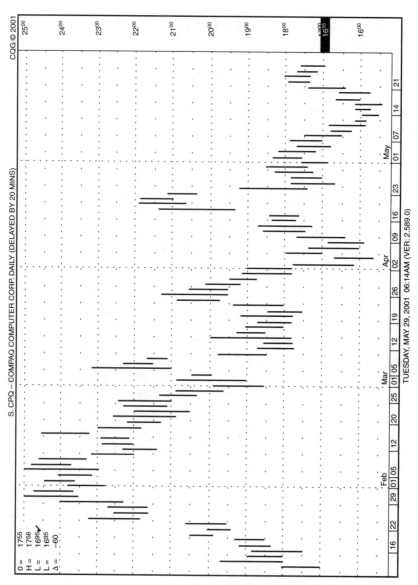

Figure 2-1. A daily price chart.

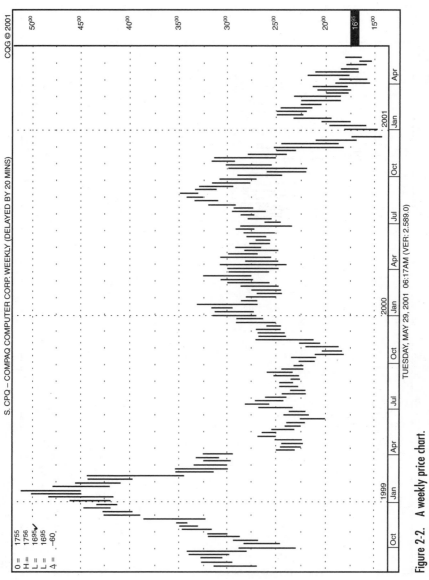

Figure 2-2. A weekly price chart.

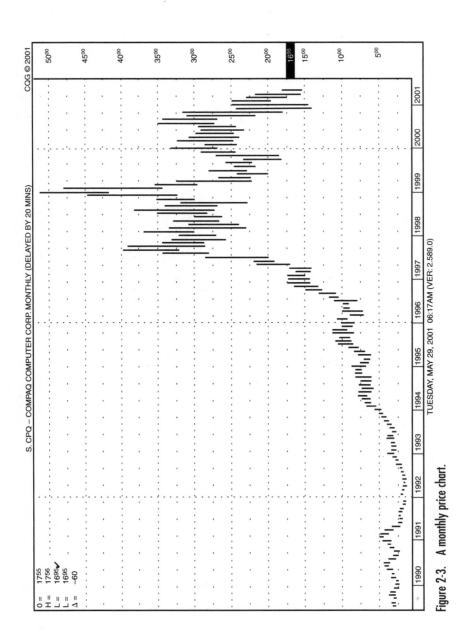

Figure 2-3. A monthly price chart.

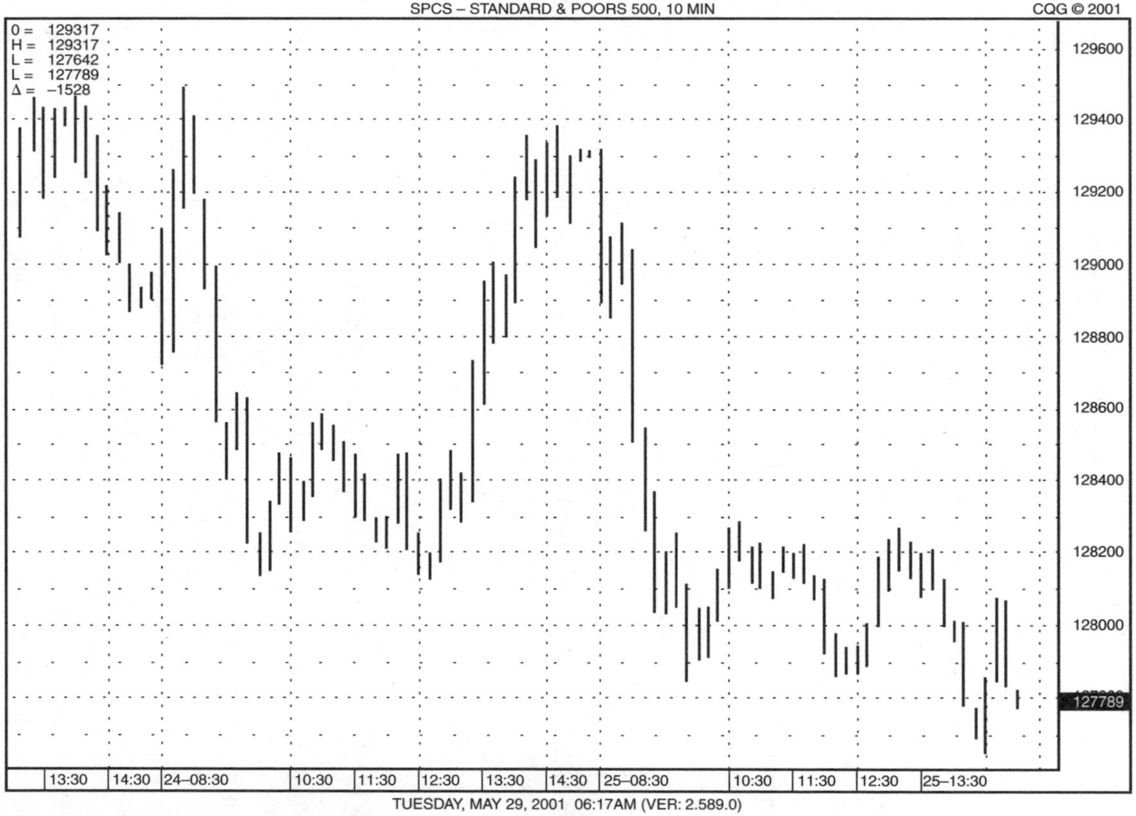

Figure 2-4. An intraday ten-minute price chart.

Most important, stock charts are useful because they are the basis of many *timing indicators*. Timing indicators are the tools we use to determine the exact times to buy and sell stocks. Charting tools allow us to view such indicators in relation to the price of a stock and tell us when a stock is starting to move up or down.

The history of the stock chart dates back to the rice market of sixteenth-century Japan. There are many types of charts. You may be familiar with some of these, while you may never have seen other types of charts before. Chart types include bar charts, candlestick charts, point-and-figure charts, wave charts, Renko charts, and Kaji charts. The most common type of chart used in stock trading, and the one you should definitely familiarize yourself with, is the open-high-low-close bar chart (sometimes abbreviated as OHLC). See Figures 2-1 through 2-4.

How to Read Charts

Figure 2-1 illustrates the daily bar chart. This is an OHLC type daily bar chart. Each individual bar shows the daily price movement of the stock. In this type of chart, the opening price for the day is indicated by the mark on the left of the bar. The daily high is indicated by the top of the bar and the daily low is indicated by the bottom of the bar. The day's closing price (or last traded price) is indicated by the mark on the right of the bar. The time frame for this chart is three months, so there should be sixty-four bars (one for each of the sixty-four trading days in a three-month period). Weekends and holidays are not included in such charts.

KEEPING THINGS SIMPLE AND EFFECTIVE

Investors are constantly bombarded with information. News, commercial advertisements, and entertainment have pervaded our everyday lives for over a century. With the advent of the Internet, even our computers have become channels through which we can receive information (however useless much of it may be). And there is no lack of information directed toward stock traders and investors. Television channels such as Bloomberg and CNBC are completely dedicated to informing us about the financial world. This is what Chimp Jacob and I do on our Web site as well. We give opinions and information that we feel are important to you.

Given the plethora of information out there, what should you believe in? We've already discussed a method for deciding what information you should and should not pay attention to (if you don't remember, check out the section in Chapter 1 called "Can You Believe What You See on the Internet and on TV?"). We haven't told you to stop listening to reports about stocks, but we have told you to listen to them strategically. You are better off being selective rather than attempting to acquire a vast amount of information.

Five Reasons to Keep Things Simple

Keeping things simple will put you on the road to profitable trading. By maintaining simplicity you can refine your trading. You will improve your odds of success if you stick to the following rules:

1. *Your methods will be clear.* When your friends ask you how you pick stocks, you should be able to tell them in just a few sentences, without any convoluted statements like, "I buy it when it looks good."
2. *You will have fewer expenses.* Instead of wasting money to buy over-priced trading systems, software, or other people's opinions, you will have more money to trade. You should be able to get almost all the information you need for free.
3. *You will have fewer decisions to make.* Instead of being indifferent about twenty or thirty stocks that someone else suggested to you, you will realize which stocks are ready to be bought and which ones are not.
4. *It's less work.* This one should be self-explanatory in a world where time is money.
5. *You have less to learn.* This one goes along with number four. Less to learn means less time wasted and more opportunity to make money. It also means there's less to forget and fewer mistakes to make—always a plus.

Dancing Darvas and the Law of Diminishing Returns

Some of the most successful investors have made their fortunes with very little outside information. One memorable example of this is ballet dancer Nicholas Darvas. In his book, *How I Made $2,000,000 in the Stock Market*,[1] Darvas outlined a simple timing method he used. The remarkable part of his story is that for a number of years, he outperformed so-called market professionals and made himself a fortune.

I say that Darvas's methods were simple. But what do I mean by that? All I'm really saying is he didn't read the newspapers and he didn't watch TV to make decisions about his investments (this was before the time of the Internet). Instead, Darvas relied completely on a small amount of factual information that he analyzed on his own. He used stock charts to find stock that moved through different levels, which he called *boxes*. When

---

[1] Larchmont, NY: American Research Council, 1980.

one of the stocks he was following moved up into a new level, he would buy it. When it moved back down through the previous level, he would sell. It's that simple and that effective.

The details of Darvas's story are not important. What we can learn from it, however, is that sometimes less is more. If you remember your economics, think of the law of diminishing returns. It is by no means good to have a lack of information. You need to know about certain things: prices, trading volume, timing indicators, etc. But there is a point at which having more information begins to help you less, or even begins to hinder your performance.

Testing Your Methods for Simplicity

When scientists develop hypotheses, they don't usually make broad statements that will be hard to prove. When they conduct experiments, they include only the variables that will prove or disprove their claims. It should be the same when you implement your trading methods.

Get out a pen and paper. Can you write down in a sentence or two how you determine whether to buy or sell a stock? If so, write it down. Then, make a list below that statement. This list should include all the pieces of information you need to make your system work. What kinds of things should your list include? Facts and concrete information are best. Check Chapter 1 for our definition of a fact, if you're still a little unclear. Your list can and should include things like price charts, timing tools, trend, risk, and so on.

If you still don't have a trading method, don't worry. You'll soon learn tools with which you can develop your own method. Once you do develop your investing technique, come back to this exercise and *do it again*! It will help you determine if your method is simple enough.

TRADING ON MARGIN

Make money to use money. This is the goal and definition of capitalism. The more money you have access to, the easier it should be to make more. It makes sense, too. If I've got $1 and I make another dollar by investing that dollar, that means that I've made a 100 percent profit. That's a huge profit, and it's pretty unlikely that I'll make that much.

If I've got $5, though, and I make $1, that's only a 20 percent profit. Twenty percent is a little more reasonable. By having $5, it just became a lot easier and a lot more likely for me to make $1. Margin gives traders and investors access to more money. Using this extra leverage in the right way can help increase your profits. But if you don't know how to use margin, you can easily get burned.

The Power of Margin

Margin is a kind of trading power. If you have 50 percent margin (which is the standard amount of margin for stock trading accounts), you have access to twice as much money as you have in your account. If you have put $5000 in your account, you can trade with $10,000, using margin. In some types of trading, margin can be even more powerful. Futures traders, for example, pay as little as 1 or 2 percent margin. With $5000, futures traders can even buy over $1,000,000 worth of commodities. Although the stock trader is taking a significantly smaller risk than this when trading on margin, the risk is still present and should be understood.

What You Can and Can't Do with Margin

Most stocks can be bought on margin. However, some stocks cannot be bought on margin due to rules imposed by the Securities and Exchange Commission (SEC), the government agency that oversees and enforces stock trading rules and regulations. Your broker may require that your account meet specific requirements before you are able to buy on margin. In some cases, the SEC may disallow the use of margin on some stocks in order to prevent traders from speculating too actively in these stocks.

How Margin Can Burn You

Margin is a tool that can make trading easier as well as more profitable. You can trade twice as many shares when you use margin because you have more buying power. But buying power has its negative side as well (as you will see shortly). Having more buying power will also give you access to higher-priced stocks. But with that additional buying power comes responsibility as well. The money you use for margin is a loan from your benevolent broker. Margin is *not* a free ride. In fact, for every dollar of margin you use, you pay interest. The money doesn't fall like manna from heaven. It belongs to your broker. And don't be fooled into thinking that your broker is lending you the money because he or she loves you. The broker has an ulterior motive. It's called the profit incentive. It's also known as capitalism.

You are charged interest on the margin you use. If you aren't making enough money on your margin trades to cover the interest and trading fees, then you shouldn't be using margin to begin with! Before you use margin, be sure to check the interest rates your broker charges to let you borrow this money. If you're worried about whether trading stocks on margin has been having a serious impact on your profits, you should be able to check the damages on your account statement.

Margin Call: The Investor's Nightmare

Worse than paying interest for trading on margin is the *margin call*. This phenomenon occurs because of the rules of margin trading, which specify that a minimum balance (usually about $2000) must be maintained if you wish to trade on margin. When your actual cash account balance falls below this amount, your broker will issue a margin call.

This is a notice to you that if you do not sell some of your margin position within a given amount of time (normally a day or two), your broker will sell stocks in your portfolio for you. If you do not take the initiative and sell stocks on your own, your broker can sell anything in your portfolio he or she wishes. This can seriously impact your long-term investment strategy.

BUY LOW AND SELL HIGH
OR BUY HIGH AND SELL HIGHER?
TWO WAYS TO PLAY THE GAME

We've all heard stories about the lucky few that bought stocks like Microsoft when they were worth only a few dollars a share. But these people are by far in the minority of those who have been successful in the stock market. Of course, these stories capture our attention for several reasons. First, the strategies used by these individuals were straightforward and simple. They simply invested in a company at a low price, and watched it grow. It seems that these people did not have to do much research and analysis and simply picked winners at very low prices.

But investing in inexpensive stocks is not nearly as easy as those stories would lead you to believe. In fact, you are much more likely to make money by investing in the stock of well-established companies, rather than throwing your money at a bunch of cheapies and hoping one of them turns into a Microsoft. This is not to say that there is no room for investing in low-priced stocks. In Chapter 5 we will discuss in-depth strategies for successfully investing in low-priced stocks. In this section, we'll explain the pros and cons of buying low/selling high and buying high/selling higher.

Buying Low and Selling High: The Dreamer's Game

If you don't care to learn realistic and profitable methods of investing in the stock market, this strategy might just be for you. There are literally hundreds of thousands of low-priced and penny stocks out there. Pick the right one, and you could make 1000 percent profit, if not more. Pick the wrong one, and maybe you only lose a few hundred bucks. So, what's the problem? It's that you're probably more likely to lose a few hundred bucks here and there, until you've just about wasted all the money you started with. The likelihood that you will make a huge profit on these types of stocks is extremely low. Don't get caught up in this game.

There are more realistic ways of investing in low-priced stocks, but these methods (like all realistic methods of investing) take time and discipline to succeed. Even though it may have seemed like a very short time in which those people who invested in Microsoft made their millions, it more likely took at least a decade and some very tempting second-guessing. If you ask some of these early investors how they decided to invest in Microsoft, they will probably tell you it was chance or luck. Still, more likely than not, it took some skill and effort to find the right stock, buy it, and hold it. With the tools that we will give you in the second part of this book, you too can find the right stocks. But the challenge comes in having the discipline to sit on your hands and be confident that the investment decisions you make today are the ones you will be happy with ten years down the road.

Buying High and Selling Higher: The Base Hit

I am by no means a big baseball fan, so I'm a little apprehensive about using baseball analogies. But bear with me and I think you will come to a better understanding of the topic at hand. Everybody likes to hit a home run. It's great: You get to run the bases and you score a run for your team. Who doesn't want to be a big shot? But then again, where would the team be without players who hit a lot of base hits? Somebody has to get the players out on base so that when Sammy comes to bat he can hit a grand slam.

In the stock market game, taking a few little steps forward often is much more beneficial than taking a giant leap once in a great while. The problem is, there's nothing sexy and exciting about base hits. Who wants to hear that you made another couple hundred bucks trading Motorola in your IRA when he or she could be listening to Uncle Jack's story about making a cool and fast grand? Jack told you he bought a $2 stock he heard about on a tip from his girlfriend's sister's hairdresser's uncle who works for someone doing business with the respectable firm of Fleecem and Pierce. Ask Jack how many times he screwed up and lost money before he got to gloat over this trade, and he might not want to answer you.

The point is, if you already know that a company is making profits and has a solid business model, why look for others? Yes, it may be easier to buy a few thousand shares of that $2 stock, but your odds of success with such stocks is relatively low.

This is where buying high and selling higher comes in. What exactly do we mean by *high*? We don't mean dot-com stock high, as in several thousand times earning and $180 per share high. We do mean the stock of a company with reasonable earnings per share (something you will learn about in the second part of this book), and trading at about 75 to 50 percent off its highest price. Confused yet? Let's backtrack a little.

"Reputable" companies often have a much more stable trading range than smaller, less well-established companies. Also, larger stocks are more likely to give the price movement you need to make a profit. Consider these two cases. In one case, a $2 stock moves up $5 to $7. In the second case, a $50 stock moves $5 to $55. Which move is more likely to occur? Which move should be easier for you to predict and capitalize on? Both stocks have moved up $5 in share price. However, a $2 stock rising $5 in price is more than a 200 percent move, while a $50 stock rising $5 is only a 10 percent move. It is much more likely for our second case to occur. You should also have an easier time predicting and profiting from such moves.

Compared to the $2 stock, $50 per share may seem a bit steep. But remember our baseball analogy. It is easier and safer to try for a base hit than to swing for a home run and miss most of the time. If you can make $100 or $200 trading Motorola for $3 moves every few weeks, and if you can do so consistently, month after month, then you've made a few thousand dollars at the end of a year. Not too shabby. Remember Uncle Jack and his cool thousand? He may very well have lost all his profits on his next trade. If you can make yourself a few thousand extra dollars every year, do it. Don't be tempted by greed. Losing your good judgment will encourage you to make trades that expose you to unnecessary risk. More often than not, that risk will come back to haunt you as a loss.

SUMMARY

Every investor must know the basic terms and tools we will use when discussing stocks. Here is a list of the words and concepts we introduce in this chapter:

- *Buy High/Sell Higher: A good goal for the individual investor.* This goal is more reasonable and realistic than buying low and selling high, because making many small gains in well-established stocks is usually easier than making one or two huge gains in small, unknown stocks.
- *Buy Low/Sell High: The unrealistic stock investor's goal.* Although this goal is closer to traditional views of investing, it is quite hard to achieve.
- *Dollars per Share: How many dollars each share will cost you.* When one says a stock is at 20, this is a short way of saying $20 per share.

- *Lot: 100 shares of a stock.* This is the normal minimum amount of shares to be bought or sold.
- *Margin: Money that your broker may let you borrow to allow you more trading power.* Most personal stock trading accounts allow 50 percent margin, which means you can use twice the amount of your cash balance to buy and sell stocks.
- *Margin Call: When your balance falls below the minimum requirement for margin trading.* When your broker issues a margin call on your account, you must sell (liquidate) some of your stock (to meet margin requirements) within a stated amount of time, or the brokerage firm will do it for you.
- *Odd Lot: Any amount of shares under 100.* An odd lot may be anywhere from one share to ninety-nine shares of stock. Buying and selling odd lots can be useful to the investor with limited resources.
- *OHLC Chart: Open-high, low-close chart.* This is the most common type of stock chart, and the one you should be familiar with. On a daily OHLC chart, the top and bottom of each bar represent the daily high and low, respectively, while the left notch represents opening price and the right notch represents closing price.
- *Price Chart: A graph on which the historical prices of a stock are plotted.* Charts come in many forms and help investors and traders gain a better perspective on recent and historical price movements. You can get charts for free at many financial Web sites.
- *Share: The basic unit of a stock.* Shares are pieces of ownership in a company, which are bought and sold on a stock exchange according to the laws of supply and demand.
- *Simplicity: Keeping your investment strategy simple is keeping it effective.* If you can't recall why, be sure to reread the section, "Five Reasons to Keep Things Simple."
- *Total Share Cost: (price per share) × (number of shares) = total share cost*

3

THE DOS AND DON'TS OF PICKING WINNING STOCKS

"People are inexterminable—like flies and bed-bugs. There will always be some that survive in cracks and crevices—that's us."

Robert Frost

Picking stocks that make money is not a difficult task if you follow a few basic rules and procedures. This chapter will introduce you to some of the dos and don'ts.

A FEW BASIC KEYS THAT WILL HELP YOU PICK WINNING STOCKS

Let's face it; trading in stocks can be a risky proposition. The market is like a jungle. Survival of the fittest reigns supreme. We can approach the markets like a lion or a tiger, attempting to bully our way to profits by using brute force and power, or we can be like the speedy monkey, darting from tree to tree before we get captured and take a loss.

Because we have a finite amount of money with which to trade we cannot be like the lion or tiger that has vast buying power and influence. We need to be quick and clever. This was the thought that inspired us in 1998 to create a Web site for stock investors. We call the service 2chimps.com as our way of saying that we are all market monkeys from time to time.

Being a "market monkey" can have its upside as well as its downside. On the positive side we like to think of the monkey as agile, clever, keen, perceptive, opportunistic, quick to react, and an effective strategist, particularly in emergencies. The negative side of being a market monkey is that, at times, we tend to think like the rest of the herd. This "monkey see—monkey do" mentality is what we try to avoid at all costs since it often does little more than get us into trouble.

Humor us as we play along with the market monkey concept. With this analogy in mind, let's look at a few ways in which a clever chimp can pick winning stocks. By now, even the most simple simian may have realized that there are as many stocks listed on the Nasdaq, NYSE, and ASE as there are trees in the jungle. And that abundance of stocks makes things more than a little confusing when you try to decide which stocks are likely to make you a bundle of bananas.

Before dipping your toes into the dangerous market jungle waters, it's crucial that you understand how to tell a good stock from a bad stock, a possible winner from a loser, a turkey from a tech stock. After all, it's a waste of time and energy to climb a tree only to find that there's no fruit! So whether you have decided to trade from your computer or you find the television and newspaper more convenient, this chapter will help you navigate the columns of numbers, abbreviations, and market lingo of stock research. Don't be intimidated. This process is simple and easily learned.

Many Ways to Pick

There are many ways to pick winning stocks. There are even more ways to pick losing stocks. Most investors have no trouble picking losers. The trick is to pick winners. Some investors pick winners and then turn them into losers by having a poor trading plan. The simple fact that you are able to pick winning stocks doesn't mean that you will be able to make money on them. Picking stocks that have the potential to win is only the first part of the key to success. Once you have picked a stock you have to carry out your plan correctly. If you can't follow the plan then your potential winner will become a loser, and you'll end up like many of the market monkeys—frustrated and broke. Once you "pick 'em" you've got to "play 'em" correctly.

There are literally hundreds of ways in which stocks can be picked. Most losing ways fall into one category, and most winning ways fall into a few categories. The losing ways are essentially such haphazard techniques as guessing, picking stocks because the name sounds good (might as well throw darts), taking tips from friends or relatives, asking brokers for advice, listening to the advice of analysts on television, consulting a fortune teller, playing a hunch, or using Tarot cards.

As an alternative, you can do your own research. Chief Chimp Jacob and I suggest that doing your own research will bring you the best results, particularly if you follow the methods taught in this book. The ability to pick good stocks can be learned. You, the individual investor, are encouraged to do your own research (whether investing in stocks or mutual funds) and to benefit from the fruits of your labor. Doing your own research will also promote a greater level of control and understanding of your stock portfolio. Let's take a look at what's wrong with many of the popular ways of picking stocks.

The Television Investment Guru

If you're new to investing or trading and uncertain as to which method(s) of stock selection to use, then financial analysts, market gurus, and stock pickers on business television will likely impress you with their vast amounts of wisdom, giving you and a lot of other people their "money-making" advice free of charge. Don't let the Wall Street, business-suited baboons fool you! More often than not you'll pay a heavy price for taking their "free" market advice.

Why? The simple fact is that they will often be as wrong as they are right. In other words, their batting average may be about the same as what you can achieve by random selection. What's wrong with this picture? Aren't there any real experts out there? Don't any of them know what they're talking about? If they're not real experts then how did they get on television? Isn't it illegal to represent yourself as an expert if you're not?

If you look a little closer at the names of TV analysts, you'll notice that they are actually stockbrokers, fund managers, or other people who have control over a large amount of money. So it's only logical that they will take whatever chance they can to make those stocks they've chosen to invest in move a little more. The problem with doing what the analyst says is that as soon as the stock's price is jacked up enough, the big guys get out.

The hard-earned bananas of the individual chimp are sacrificed to make the portfolios of fund manager baboons look that much better. In the end, the individual trader learns nothing from following the advice of the big guys other than not to listen to them. You always learn better if you make your own mistakes; then you'll know just why you made those mistakes.

Also, watch out for apes and gorillas that go on TV claiming to be independent. Always be wary of what they say. They may be recommending stocks because they are somehow affiliated with those companies. We would not imply that these people are doing anything illegal by touting these stocks; however, it is always good to be aware that there could be any number of reasons that a stock is promoted to a general audience.

What's Wrong with Trading on Tips?

You already know that doing your own research is the best way to pick stocks. But you might not understand why it's better than taking tips. You trust your friends, so if your buddy tells you about a stock he's having the time of his life with, what ulterior motive could he have? He's not the stockbroker or fund manager we mentioned before. He's not on CNBC getting national exposure while telling you to buy stocks he's already in. But if you buy stocks your friends are doing well in, you're making a big mistake.

Buying stocks on tips leads to the whipsaw effect. It sounds bad enough, but it's even worse when it's happening to you. Imagine that you're talking to your monkey buddy at a party. He tells you that he's doing really well in Ben and Jerry's stock. He bought it because they now produce Chunky Monkey ice cream, a chimp favorite. Ben and Jerry's is up 40 percent from where he bought it. He also says that if his capital weren't tied up in other places, he'd probably buy more. So you decide to quit monkeying around and buy in as well.

You buy in at 60. Since you have just started trading, and you only have a few thousand dollars in your account, this is a somewhat expensive stock for you. You don't really feel comfortable with your money in it. But, what the hell, your friend is one of the smartest simians you know. Right? Well, he's already made his money so here's the real question: Did you do the smart thing or did you buy into a story stock at the height of its move?

You watch as your stock climbs a few more points, and you figure if it went up 40 percent for your friend, it can go up 40 percent for you too. Too bad, Ben and Jerry's stock has had its run and soon it drops 15 points. Your friend still gets out at a profit, but you bought at an inflated price. You sell because you're frustrated. You end up with nothing but rotten bananas.

You check the stock again a few days later, and it has recovered 10 of the 15 points it lost during its last drop. Seeing this, you want revenge. You could have already made back two-thirds of your lost money. So you buy back in the hope of regaining lost capital. Soon, the rally ends and you lose even more money when the stock returns to noninflated prices. You've just made the same mistake for the second time. You bought high and sold lower, ignoring a cardinal rule of trading.

Now let's do a little analysis of this situation. The first mistake you made was trading on a tip from a friend. Had you found the stock and watched it a little, you would have realized that the price was inflated. Instead, you made mistake number two. You bought it because your emotions told you that you might be missing a chance to make money. And, when the stock was at its low, you made your third mistake. You sold at a low. Emotions told you to go against the old trading rule, "Buy low, sell high."

This example could go on and on, but I'm sure that by now, you get the picture. Finding your own stocks allows for the deepest level of understanding of what is in your portfolio and why it's there. And, understanding why you bought stocks prevents panicking as well as problems such as the whipsaw effect.

Where the Heck Do I Find Hot Stocks Anyway?

Everybody's seen them, and most people have no idea what they are! Trying to understand *The Wall Street Journal* can be scary. Those columns upon columns of small type, all arranged in some cryptic order may seem incomprehensible, requiring an advanced degree in order to understand the information. Well, let me dispel that fear! First of all, you'll never need to know what half of those numbers mean in the first place, and, second, you may never need to look at those lists to pick stocks at all!

When picking stocks, it is critical to have an up-to-date newspaper or access to a reliable financial Web site. Buy *The Wall Street Journal* or *The Financial Times* if you're more print-oriented. You should be able to find these publications at any newsstand, convenience store, etc. Most major newspapers, such as *The New York Times* or the *Chicago Tribune* will have information on stocks in the financial section. But remember not to read too much of the junk they publish there, because you don't want to let "professionals" pick your stocks for you.

If you're familiar with computers, access CNBC Online (http://www.cnbc.com), CNNFN (http://www.cnnfn.com) or Bloomberg (http://www.bloomberg.com). You might also want to check out bigger online brokers such as Datek (http://www.datek.com) or E*TRADE (http://www.etrade.com), which often offer free delayed quotes as well as timely news stories, charts, and some other useful goodies.

When using a financial newspaper for picking stocks, look for the "Most Actives" list. This is a list of stocks that have had the highest trading volume (number of shares traded) for the day or week. It's usually found at the end of the stock price tables.

Many financial Web sites have the same "Most Actives" lists as financial publications. Sometimes they will be hidden in summaries of daily market activity, so you'll have to do a little digging through the babble to find names and symbols. They might be disguised under names like "Big Movers," and so on.

There are also other lists, such as "Winners and Losers," which records stocks that have seen the biggest percent gains and losses over a given time period. Some Web sites provide stock screens. These are searches with predefined parameters, such as stock price, value, or growth, technical indicator breakouts, etc. These tools may be a little hard for you to understand, and it might be better to stick to the simpler lists. But when you have been better educated about trading, these tools will help you find stocks that fit your personal investment objectives.

Getting information on stocks can be fun and exciting. And, in this day and age, there is loads and loads of information out there. You could spend an entire day checking statistics on a stock, researching performance, analyzing its charts and comparing it to other stocks in its industry. But don't get too hung up on one stock. Do some research, take some notes, and note the stock's symbol. Then, move on to the next stock.

It's only natural that when a hungry chimp finds bananas, he or she wants to eat them right away. But even inexperienced monkeys know that unripe bananas are no fun. Try to keep a list of between ten and twenty symbols that you've found and check them once every day or two. Don't jump in right away, for fear of unripe bananas. And, always remember not to check stocks too much. Emotional chimps don't make good traders.

Should I Like Every Stock on the "Hot Stocks" List?

Every sector and every industry is going to have its winners and losers. But just as some parts of the jungle have more banana trees than others do, not all industries are equal. Some industries are perpetually hot. Rarely will there be a time when you cannot find a number of big movers in these groups. However, trading in some categories can be costly or too risky. If a tech stock can gain 20 points in half a day, it can be lost just as quickly (if not quicker)! Likewise, there are groups that don't move much (similar to industries, which are quiet most of the time), and then make big moves several times a year.

Two major "hot" sectors for many months have been technology and medical stocks. If you're ready for a ride, check out some of these stocks. When you search through the "Hot Stocks" lists, you'll come across all sorts of stocks. There will be financials, service providers (e.g., airlines), manufacturers (e.g., car makers, clothing), oil companies, and diversified holding companies, among others. Be selective.

It may be a very wise decision to invest in traditional stocks. They often offer stable, steady growth. However, the 3 to 7 percent returns you get might not be quite the thrill you're looking for. And that's why it's a hungry chimp's job to search for stocks in the more volatile sectors and keep a close eye on them.

WHAT'S A TECH STOCK?

If you watch the news or read the paper, you've probably heard the hype. You've heard about initial public offerings (IPOs—when a stock can first be traded by the public) that have increased in worth by 500 percent in only a few days of trading. Or a little-known Internet company that makes news and becomes every trader's dream. A stock that can gain 50 percent of your portfolio in a few months instead of over a lifetime has become a real possibility. And it is all due to the technology sector.

Technology stocks that the average chimp should consider trading are on both the NYSE and the Nasdaq stock exchange. Stocks on the NYSE are usually more established companies. They are required to have certain earning standards and other qualifications.

There are many high-quality technology stocks on the NYSE. There, you will find computer manufacturers, semiconductor (chip) manufacturers, telecom and wireless communication companies. These companies tend to have longer histories, more stable price growth, and less share turnover. This is not to say, however, that NYSE technology stocks cannot make and/or lose a chimp big bucks.

The Nasdaq is the exchange with more speculative stocks. It has less stringent requirements for listing. Often Nasdaq stocks show large earnings deficits. However, in today's crazy market, many stocks on the Nasdaq are valued without regard to current earnings, but with the belief in future earnings. Technology stocks on the Nasdaq come in a wide range of flavors and colors. There are technology consulting firms, Business to Business (B2B) Web sites, Business to Consumer (B2C) Web sites, Internet Service Providers (ISP), software manufacturers, chip and computer manufacturers, high-tech device manufacturers, and so on. You name it, and the Nasdaq has probably got it!

Since the late 1980s, many high-tech firms and Internet-based businesses have made IPOs on the Nasdaq. Speculators and investors alike have gobbled up these stocks, causing larger price fluctuations than have ever been seen in the U.S. stock market. It's still not too late for you to jump in. There's always a technology stock that's ready to take off, and one that's ready to plummet. Soon you'll learn how to find out which ones to buy.

WHAT'S A MEDICAL STOCK?

Medical stocks tend to be some of the biggest movers in today's market. And medicals follow the same rules as techs do as far as the NYSE and Nasdaq are concerned. NYSE medical stocks are mostly larger established drug manufacturers such as Pfizer and Eli Lilly. They may also include medical labs like Abbott Labs. NYSE medical stocks can move quickly, however, and provide the average investor with a greater chance of long-term capital appreciation.

Nasdaq medical stocks also include drug companies and medical labs, but most of the companies on the Nasdaq exchange tend to be cutting-edge and deal with more experimental technology. The buzzword for some Nasdaq medicals is "biotech." Biotech companies develop drugs, medical processes, and devices that harness the power of genes to cure human disease or improve biological products (plants and animals). These stocks have been known to move just as rapidly as Internet and technology sector stocks and come with the same risks of rapid, large, and often unexpected price savings.

WHAT'S AN IPO?

In order to help you understand what an IPO (initial public offering) is, I'm going to tell you a story. Suppose that I designed a banana that connects to the Internet using coconut shells as antennas. I created a company called Bananasoft, got a patent for the device, and had a few prototypes produced. I sold the items I had produced, but I had to pay for them with my own funds! Every investor I talked to thought that Bananasoft was worth developing so I decided to look for some investors.

Chimps with lots of money are called *venture capitalists*. They are always looking for primates with a vision, and that's me. So they gave me a bunch of money to improve my Internet banana and produce more of them. As soon as the new line of Bananasoft products hit the stores, the public responded enthusiastically! Everyone loved my products and soon I was raking in the cash.

But I knew that if I had access to even more money, I could expand my business to produce Internet banana accessories, as well as a full line of electronic bug removal devices, which every chimp would own and love. So my lawyers convinced Central Congo Bancorp (the biggest bank in the jungle) to help me offer an IPO for Bananasoft. In doing this, I sold parts of my company as shares to the public, and I gained even more money to reinvest in research and development as well as production.

The IPO Process Involves Three Steps

First, the private owners of the company must find a bank or brokerage firm to "take the company public" (the bank or brokerage is called the *underwriter*). In other words, the company doesn't initially have the means or capital to offer shares to the public all by itself, so the underwriters help it. In my story, Central Congo Bancorp became the underwriter for the IPO of Bananasoft.

In the second step, the underwriters become responsible for the advertising, pricing, and legal proceedings of the IPO. They decide on how much stock to offer (this number may range from a few million shares to over a hundred million shares) as well as a price per share they believe to be fair. Normally, it is hard for the general public to buy shares at this point. Shares are offered to company employees, executives, lawyers, underwriters, preferred clients, and anyone else who has a connection to the company. Individual investors usually must file applications and be approved to own shares during this phase.

Finally, as the third step, a date and time are set for the stock to begin trading on an exchange. Bananasoft was lucky. On its first day of trading on the CHMPDAQ exchange, it went from an initial price of $8 to $25. That's over 200 percent gain—spectacular! In today's market, IPOs like this are possible.

But many market monkeys believe that this is the way all IPOs act. This couldn't be further from the truth. The thousands of IPOs you don't hear about may have had mediocre or even poor performance in the initial hours and days of trading. It is very possible that you will lose money trading new stocks!

Chief Chimp Jacob and I both believe that it is important to analyze a stock's price and trading history before deciding to trade. With no price history, IPOs are on our list of the riskiest trades. Furthermore, in an emotionally charged environment such as the first few trading hours of a new stock, most traders (including even the most experienced old apes) find themselves letting their stomachs and not their minds control their trades.

In addition to the above dos and don'ts for stock picking, there are various other specific methods that we will teach you. Everything we have told you until now is not nearly as specific as we'd like it to be. If you're going to be a successful market monkey then you need to be a good strategist, knowing which vines to swing from and which to avoid. Once we dispose of a few more basics, like picking a stock broker or brokerage firm, we'll be ready to test the waters of technical analysis as a specific means of picking stocks.

SUMMARY

This chapter taught the basics of stock picking. Here are the basic dos and don'ts of stock picking.

Do:
- Conduct your own research.
- Check *The Wall Street Journal* or the *Financial Times* for "most active" stocks.
- Find a few other indicators that you think make a stock "hot" and look for them (we'll discuss indicators later on).

Don't:
- Be swayed by the charm of the investment guru.
- Buy and sell according to your friends' and family's recommendations.
- Listen to other stock "tips."

When picking stocks and making your investment decisions, remember one thing: Make them on your own. Your friend might be trying to help you in telling you to buy or sell his or her favorite stocks. But your own opinion and research are the most important.

C H A P  E R

PICKING A STOCKBROKER

"Small service is true service while it lasts."
William Wordsworth

Stockbrokers come in many shapes and sizes. Some act as nothing more than a tool to receive the independent chimp's stock orders. Others play a very active role in the investment strategy of their clients. Still others act as salespeople and can become very obnoxious and pushy.

Deciding what kind of broker is right for you can be a difficult undertaking, especially if you have no prior investing experience. Should you get an electronic broker first or wait a while? Do you want investment advice and stock ratings from your broker? Perhaps the two most important considerations are what makes you comfortable and what seems the most convenient. Don't be discouraged if your first broker or even your first several brokers don't work out. Be careful whom you pick to help you invest your hard-earned bananas.

IF YOU'RE READY TO TRADE

So you've decided you're ready to trade. You've got some risk capital, you've got some knowledge, and now you need an account. What are your choices? Nowadays, the major decision is to choose between online or traditional brokerage. Most online brokerages are considered discount brokerages because they offer low trade commissions and they don't contact you often. If you've decided to use an online brokerage, then read on.

Where to Look

Names of popular online brokerage firms can be found in newspapers, television, magazines, and on the Internet. If you want a fairly comprehensive list of reputable online brokers, check out an Internet directory such as Yahoo!. Try looking in the Financial Services section for "Brokerage Firms" or "Brokerage Houses" and then under the "Electronic" or "Online" subcategory.

What to Look For

There are several major factors you should consider when choosing a brokerage firm. First of all, many brokerages have minimum starting account balances that you must meet in order to open an account. Depending on which firm you choose, this requirement may be as low as $500. And, depending on how much risk capital you have, this may be a major factor in opening an account.

Another very important factor is commission rates. If you have an account with a small amount of capital, it's important to keep commission rates as low as you can. There are several ways to do this. Some brokerage firms advertise extremely low commission rates, but you may notice that once you've signed up you're not getting those rates.

This may be due to the fact that those low rates are usually special offers. They apply to people who have a certain balance in their account, people who trade more than a certain number of times in a given time period, and so on. Before you set up your account, call the brokerage firm and actually talk to a broker. Try to bargain, and see if they can set up a lower commission rate for you.

Some stock brokerages offer more than others. And contrary to what your logic might tell you, the more expensive brokers don't always offer more services. That's why it's important to shop around. Some brokerages will offer free real-time quotes, while others may charge a fee for quotes or require certain trading activity to receive them. Others may offer the option of automated telephone trading as well as the option of placing orders over the phone.

Also offered may be investment information services, which could help the average chimp learn about the basics of using a broker, investing, as well as news services and other catchy benefits. If you're a big traveler, some brokers offer airline "miles" for trading or discounts on credit cards linked to banks associated with the brokerage firms. Check around; there's no shortage of deals that could save you big bucks.

WHY ARE COMMISSION COSTS SO IMPORTANT?

To put it simply, it's all relative. Let's pretend that I open an account with an initial balance of $10,000. The starting commission rate at my brokerage firm is $20 per trade. When I make one trade, I'm spending .02 percent (or $20) of the money in my account to make that trade. However if I have $500, it's a different story. Making one trade with a $20 commission requires that I spend 4 percent of the money in my account for every trade. That means that unless I make more than an average of $20 per trade, I will only be able to make twenty-five trades or fewer before I spend all the money in my account!

DO YOU NEED ALL THE FREE STUFF?

Not at all! Of course it's nice to have free stuff. And, you might be really jealous when you see your coworkers taking advantage of their real-time, streaming quote, or trading right from their desk. However, too much information is more distracting than you may realize. Brokerage firms exist to generate commissions by executing your trades. As we've said before, you should be the one making the decisions about your trades, not brokers, not analysts, and, above all, not your emotions. So when you decide not to overstimulate yourself with loads of information, you are actually doing yourself a favor and making it easier to win the game.

WHAT'S THE DIFFERENCE?

There are two major categories of brokerages: full-service and discount. Increasingly, banks offer investment services as well, so if transferring money from account to account isn't your cup of tea, try asking about this at your local bank.

Choose your brokerage firm according to your style of investment. Ask yourself if you would feel better with an investment adviser and/or broker on the other end of the phone, or if you would feel just as confident without even talking to a person at all.

Full-Service Brokers

Full-service brokerages serve several purposes. First and foremost, they act as the go-between for buyers and sellers of stocks (this is the major purpose of any brokerage firm). Second, they act as a resource for individual investors. If you sign up with a full-service broker, don't be surprised if some baboon gives you a call to tell you about hot stocks in which you should invest your bananas.

But be aware that these baboons are often like used-tree-house salespeople; they may have ulterior motives. Your stockbroker may be asking you to buy a stock, which his or her brokerage firm is trying to move "off the shelves." This would occur when your brokerage firm has been involved in the public offering of a company, or has a large number of shares that it needs to get off of its hands. In fact, brokerage houses often pay their brokers bonuses to push stocks like these.

If you've signed up with a full-service broker, don't start hooting and hollering just yet. The stocks your full-service broker will tell you about will not always be "good" or "bad," nor will they usually be stocks the firm has asked them to move. But always keep in mind that one of our cardinal rules of investing is that a market monkey should choose stocks for him- or herself.

Discount Brokers

Discount brokers are divided into two subcategories: discount and deep discount. Discount and, to an even greater degree, deep discount brokers primarily facilitate the buying and selling of stocks. You will practically never have discount brokers call you and tell you about a stock. However, you may receive free materials, newsletters, or investment tools to help you make decisions on investments. Be aware that if you sign up with a discount broker, you will be in an extremely independent investment decision-making environment.

The major difference between all three types of brokerages beyond service is price. Brokers make some money on commissions (a fee charged for the execution of a trade). When a stockbroker assists you in deciding what to buy or sell, there will normally be a larger commission fee than otherwise. Solicited trades (when a broker asks you to buy a stock) will also cost you more. If you don't have a lot of cash in your account to start with, try to get the lowest trading fees possible. Chimp Elliott's advice is to stick with a discount broker and make your own trading decisions once you have learned the basics of trading and order placement.

SUMMARY

Can there be any advantage to trading with a major brokerage firm and getting their advice? Is this the right thing for you? Here are some considerations on both sides of the issue. Think about them and then decide for yourself.

- *There is no hard and fast evidence that the advice of a major brokerage firm can help you make money*. In fact, many brokerage firms have downright miserable records. The recent dot-com debacle is merely one example of how most brokerage houses recommended worthless stocks when they were high in price and then advised their clients to dump those stocks after they had lost a great deal of value.

- *Even if you use a major firm you cannot expect to get perfect advice.* If you believe that the top brokers can help you make money then you're likely to be disappointed.

- *Most major brokerage firms recommend many stocks.* You'll still have to make the final decision as to which stocks you will buy or sell. And we know that most investors will choose wrong.

- *Many brokerage firm recommendations only tell you what to buy and at what price.* They rarely tell you how much to risk and when to get out if you're wrong.

- *Brokerage houses have a vested interest in recommending stocks since they make commissions when you trade.* Be careful what you believe!

- *Many brokerage houses have a conflict of interest. They are often the promoters or underwriters of the stocks they recommend.* Although they disclose this and although it's (usually) legal for them to promote stocks, they are biased and, therefore, suspect.

- *If you're a favored client of a brokerage firm (by which we mean that you have big bucks in your account) you may be given tips before the rest of the investment world finds out about a recommendation.* It's not unusual for such investors to buy before the public knows the news and then to sell when the public is buying. If you think this doesn't happen, then you're living in a fool's paradise. If you have a small account with a firm then you won't be privy to such advance information.

- *At times your brokerage firm may give you an opportunity to buy into an IPO that they are underwriting.* You could make some money this way when the IPO market is active and stocks in general are trending higher. So this could be an advantage to you.

- *Major firms often charge higher commissions.* Do you want to pay higher commissions for services you can't use?

- *Some brokers can pressure you and persuade you to make some trades and not others.* If you value your independence and are easily influenced, then consider not using a broker but rather trading online.

- *At times the amount of information available through your broker could be overwhelming.* Not all market monkeys can handle the input. Our small simian cerebrums can only handle so much input at one time.

- *Large brokerage firms can often offer you a variety of integrated services that you may not be able to obtain from an online broker.* This is something you may want to consider.

- *Some people can actually do better in their trading if they deal with a human being to take their orders.* A broker can actually help you learn things about proper procedures, order placement, and so forth.

Now let's get a little more advanced. Chapter 5 will give you a few tips and specific procedures for finding stocks that can make you money.

CHAPTER

5

TRADING
THE CHEAPIES

"We haven't the money, so we've got to think."
Ernest Rutherford

Why would anybody want to trade cheap stocks to begin with? If you've already decided to invest $10,000, you should have no problem buying a substantial number of shares in $20 or even $50 stocks. This strategy seems less risky as well; a higher-priced stock usually reflects that the company is strong and profitable, right? Not necessarily.

As we have learned from the Internet bubble as well as numerous examples before it, the fact that a stock is high-priced has no bearing on whether the company is a good investment nor does it, in any way, guarantee that the stock price will continue to rise. Taking the time to research and invest in some lower-priced stocks offers many advantages to your portfolio.

Most of all, it presents opportunities for profit from new economic growth. Whereas your friends might still be monkeying around investing in only large-cap and traditional companies, you could turn out to be the person you always hear about who put some money into a smaller company and just kept watching it grow.

Still, investing in lower-priced stocks is not for everyone. Of course, many of these issues present a greater risk to investors. In this chapter, we'll teach you how to avoid picking the rotten bananas (of which there are many). We will discuss specific, easy-to-read signs that you can look for. Finding good stocks under $10 can be challenging and tricky; these signs should help you determine whether the stocks you find are worth your money, or if they might as well be banana cream pie.

VOLUME

There are several signs to look for when determining whether a smaller stock will be a good investment. The first sign is based purely on whether other people trade the stock; this is *trading volume*. What's that? *Volume* (the word *trading* is understood when you say "volume" in reference to a stock) is simply a count of how many shares of a stock have been traded in a given amount of time.

Don't concern yourself too much with the definition; it's really very easy. If we take a look at a stock quote, we will often see the word *volume* followed by some number. Look up General Electric (symbol: GE) and locate the volume. It will be a big number, like 29,895,500. No special understanding of this number is necessary; it is just how many shares of the stock have been traded that day.

Why do we care about volume? Well, we care for two major reasons. First of all, it tells us something about the *popularity* of a particular stock. If we return to our General Electric example, 29.8 million shares is a lot. Every day, hundreds of thousands of people buy and sell General Electric's stock. Let's pretend that the average person trading General Electric stock buys or sells 100 shares (we don't know the actual information). This would mean that about 298,000 people bought or sold General Electric stock that day. This should shed some light on why stocks like GE are often referred to as widely held stocks, and should help you see how volume helps us make a judgment about the popularity of any given stocks.

The second reason we like to look at volume is to determine *liquidity*. This is just a fancy way of saying there are buyers and sellers for the stock. If a market is "liquid," I will be able to buy and sell my stock around its trading price without much trouble. If not, I may have to settle for a price drastically different from the price of the last trade.

Here's an example: I buy stock in a candy company right outside the jungle called Funky Monkey Candy Corp. Despite the company's totally hip name, monkeys just don't like candy; they prefer the fructose-filled goodness of real bananas. Funky Monkey Candy Corp. is traded on the CHIMPDAQ stock exchange. One day, I decide to get rid of my shares because all of my friends make fun of me for owning it (an extremely bad reason to sell, however). The last time Funky Monkey traded, 2000 shares were sold at $0.50. I put my order in to sell at the same price, but my shares are not sold for two weeks. Why weren't my shares sold for so long? Look at the quote we've created for Funky Monkey Candy Corp. below and try to find the daily volume.

Company Name:	Funky Monkey Candy Corp.
Dow Jones Industry:	Food Products
Exchange:	OTC
Shares Outstanding:	15,000,000
Market Cap:	9,000,000
Short Interest:	988,311
52-Week EPS:	−1.25
52-Week High:	0.73
52-Week Low:	0.21
P/E Ratio:	N/A
Yield:	N/A
Average Price:	0.34
Average Volume:	1940 (50-day)

If you've located it, you can see that it only traded 1500 shares on that day. This is an extreme example of a market without much liquidity. Stocks that are not liquid are generally not popular to begin with, and are not good ideas for investments, let alone trading.

WHO ARE THEY?

In addition to looking at volume, being informed about the company's business is important. Some hard-core technical investors may tell you otherwise, but, in the long run, a company's sector and style of business determine much of its success or failure. When researching lower-priced stocks, try to look for something unique or innovative about the company's products or services.

Does the company manufacture a product that nobody else makes? Does it consistently make improvements that can help it maintain an edge in its field? Sometimes just the fact that a company is doing research and development in emerging technologies can make it attractive. One caveat however—try not to get caught up in hype.

If you haven't found a company on your own, chances are that its price has already been somewhat inflated. Your friend or stockbroker who told you about the symbol most likely has already invested in it as well. If you haven't found the stock through your own research, it's better to consider yourself the last person to have heard about it.

NUMBER OF OUTSTANDING SHARES

When we talk about *outstanding shares*, do we mean that the shares of this company are particularly good? Well, not exactly. This is not a qualitative judgment about the shares, but when a low-priced stock has a high number of outstanding shares it may signal a good buy. In order to understand what *number of outstanding shares* means, consider two stocks.

First, we have a widely held stock like AT&T. This stock may have somewhere around 4 billion shares outstanding. That is, the number of shares of stock that the company has issued is 4 billion. Next, we have a small start-up company that has issued 84 million shares. Which company has greater potential for price fluctuations when they are both below $10?

According to the laws of supply and demand, it is much easier for a small stock to make a big move than a large stock. This is simply because there are many more shares available at any given time for a stock that has 4 billion shares outstanding than one that has only 84 million shares. Since the supply of shares is lower in the smaller stock, people who want to own the stock must settle for higher prices as they compete to buy what shares are being offered.

How can you find a stock's number of outstanding shares? Most quote services should have this information, but it requires a little digging to find. Go to cnbc.com, bigcharts.com, or your broker's Web site and type in a stock symbol. Most likely, a simple quote including price, volume, and daily change will appear.

Look for an option entitled either "advanced quote," "full quote," or "stock report" and click on it. A much larger, in-depth report should appear. Search for the number following "# outstanding shares," and you've got it. As you've probably gathered from above, the number will be big. In order to determine if this number is actually large, compare it to a widely held stock like GM. Compare it to several symbols in its own sector as well, to get a feeling for how many shares this company has issued in relation to competitors.

INSTITUTIONAL OWNERSHIP: TRADING WITH THE GORILLAS

If the term *outstanding shares* was misleading, *institutional ownership* should be no better. Is this the number of people in mental institutions and jails who own shares in a stock? Although this number may be of interest to some sociologists, this is not what institutional ownership means. This term refers to the number of shares of a company's stock that are owned by institutional investors like fund managers, pension funds, and banks. These are the people whose job it is to research, rate, and buy or sell stocks every day.

What are the pros and cons of considering institutional ownership? Of course, when a stock has high institutional ownership, that normally says something good about the long-term outlook for that stock. It basically tells us that people who have a very developed system for evaluating the long-term growth and profitability of a company consider that specific issue to be a good investment. However, institutional ownership can be a double-edged sword. If institutions own a large percent of a company and suddenly decide to sell their shares, sharp drops in stock price may result. This especially affects smaller and lower-priced stocks. Because it is easier for an institution to buy a large stake in such companies, it is also very likely that the stock price will drop dramatically if such investors choose to sell.

There are several aspects to researching institutional ownership. First of all, you can look at percent of shares owned by institutions. To find this, look back at the detailed quote you used when finding outstanding shares. You should find a tab or section entitled "institutional ownership." This will bring up a list of which institutions have a stake in this company and how big that stake is. Such institutions are required to report their holdings to the Securities and Exchange Commission (SEC), by law. Take a look at how big each owner's stake is in order to get a feeling for how much of this company is owned by institutions in general.

The second thing you might want to do is take a look at who the biggest investors in this company are. Although you may never have heard of these mutual funds and banks before, you *can* find out who they are. Morning Star is a leader in mutual fund research and offers in-depth reports for almost all mutual funds in the United States, as well as others around the world. Using their Web site (www.morningstar.com) as a resource, you can see how well funds listed as institutional owners have performed. If the largest share-holding institutions in this company have performed well in the past, it's likely that they have good reasons for buying, holding, or selling that particular stock.

INSIDER ACTIVITY

In addition to institutional owners of stocks, *insiders*, or company executives who own stock in their own company, are required by law to report their stock holdings and transactions to the SEC. So, as with institutional ownership, you should be able to easily find a list of insider activity in any detailed company report. Let's say that the chief executive officer of Funky Monkey Candy Corp. decides to sell 50,000 of his shares because he is afraid that his company is going to do poorly this quarter and he wants to have some cash for the sake of security. In order to do this, he must file forms with the SEC for the proposed sale of 50,000 shares. If he were to take any other actions on his shares, such as buying new shares or selling options on shares he currently owns (which some corporate executives do on a regular basis), he would have to report this as well.

Insiders have some of the greatest insight into the future performance of their own companies. For this reason, it is often a very prudent measure to consider what these people have done in the past several months before taking action. Especially in the case of small companies with low stock prices and a small number of outstanding shares, insider activity can be highly indicative of a company's future. If company officials believe that there is little to no hope left for their company, it would not make sense for them to hold on to shares that will eventually be worthless. Furthermore, the attitude of the company's management is reflected somewhat by insider activity. Even when a stock has a strong price, if company officers have sold their stock, this may reflect that they do not wish to be a part of their company. In other words, if the manager of a company does not want to do his or her job, how can the company even begin to succeed?

LOW-PRICED STOCKS WITH HIGH SHORT INTEREST

Looking for low-priced stocks with high short interest seems to be a method contradictory to looking at institutional ownership. In the case of institutional ownership, we look for stocks that many professional investors own because they believe them to be good investments over time. When we look for high short interest, we do basically the opposite; we are searching for stocks that many investors have bet against.

Why in the world would anyone want to do that? Mostly, we do this to catch a *short-covering rally*. If you are looking for a stock under $10, the price of this stock is likely to be significantly lower than its high. When this stock begins to move up, some of the investors who have shorted this stock are forced to buy it back, in order to either take their profits or to protect against further losses. This creates a short-covering rally, during which the price of a stock is driven up when a large number of shares, which were previously sold short, must be bought back quickly.

An example of a short-covering rally can be seen in the stock of Priceline.com (PCLN). As PCLN declined from a high of over 160, more and more investors had shorted this stock. Even as the stock approached its low of 1.06, these investors remained short, believing that Priceline.com would go broke. When the stock began to rebound along with the Nasdaq around the beginning of April 2001, some of these investors were forced to buy back those shares they had sold. In the following weeks, the price of this stock gained over 700 percent from the low of 1.06 to a peak near 7.75. This is a prime example of a short-covering rally and just how much power it has to make you money in stocks under $10.

SEX APPEAL

We've already discussed the importance of finding companies that have an innovative or exciting product. Sex appeal is a better term. However, instead of finding a specific company that is cutting edge, here we look for an entire sector or industry that is "hot." Early in the twentieth century, it was railroads; in the 1980s, it was semiconductors; in the 1990s it was computer manufacturers and then dot-com stocks. Basically, sex appeal comes down to what is popular at the moment—*zeitgeist*. Do a little test and turn on a business television show for ten minutes. Take note of which sectors are discussed the most.

Better yet, get a copy of *Time* magazine. Look at what its financial commentators are writing about. This should reveal the true *zeitgeist*; the financial commentators at *Time* must write articles about popular subjects in a relatively small amount of space. So, practically all of these articles will be discussing sectors and stocks that people consider hot.

There are two ways to play the market if you decide to make investments based on the sex appeal of different sectors. The easiest way is to select stocks using the methods discussed above, only search in sectors that currently have sex appeal. Right now, that might mean buying stocks in the biotech, technology, or energy sectors. But as does everything else nowadays, sex appeal changes fast. This is why it may be much more profitable and rewarding to try another method of using sex appeal: making predictions.

Of course, this method is riskier. However, making investments in what is going to be hot *next* is the real way to use sex appeal to make money. Do you know about an industry or technology that is just beginning to get exposure in the press? If so, it may make a better and cheaper investment than what people consider hot right now.

HOW TO BUY AND SELL STOCKS UNDER $10

Investing in stocks that cost under $10 per share is a little more tricky than investing in your average stock. Placing orders to buy and sell these types of stocks requires some strategy and some common sense. Should you use a market order, or a limit order? If you use a limit order, at what price should you enter your order?

Not every cheapie you pick will have high volume, nor will every cheapie you pick have a very large trading range. With most brokers, market orders are somewhat cheaper than limit orders. For example, with E*TRADE, market orders are between $5 and $15, depending on the exchange, while limit orders can cost up to $20. However, it is critical when trading cheap stocks (especially those with low volume or that cost under $7) that you use limit orders. For the most part, this is because when a market has limited liquidity, market orders can have unpredictable results.

Here's an example: You want to buy 1000 shares of a stock that trades 25,000 shares a day around the price of the last trade—$4.50. You enter a market order and end up getting filled at $6. Instead of spending $4500 as you had planned, you end up spending $6000 on the same amount of shares! Why can a market order make the price of a stock jump so dramatically? Because when you enter a market order, you are telling the broker that you wish to pay whatever price the lowest seller is willing to give to you.

Since the lowest offer was $6, that's what you ended up paying. If you had used a limit order and specified that you'd like to buy at $4.50, your order might not get filled right away, but you would be guaranteed that when it was filled, it would be at your price.

To the investor with a small amount of money, using limit orders to buy and sell stocks under $10 presents a dilemma. The very point of buying cheap stocks is that they allow the investor to buy more shares for a cheaper price. Using limit orders costs more and therefore decreases the ease with which you can make money on a trade.

In order for a trade to be profitable, you have to make back at least what you have spent on commissions. If you spent $20 to buy and $20 to sell, you have to make over $40 on the trade to have actually made even one cent. When buying a small amount of shares, make sure that you believe that the potential for movement in the symbol you choose to buy is high enough to cover this cost. To do this, either make sure you have bought enough shares for a small move to be profitable, or look at a price chart to determine if past moves have been large enough for you to cover at least your trading costs.

PENNY STOCKS

If low-priced stocks present a good opportunity for the individual investor to make some real profits, it would only make sense to think that penny stocks present an even better one. After all, instead of spending $1000 to buy 200 shares of a $5 stock, you could be buying 2000 shares of a fifty-cent stock. With so many shares, the price of penny stock only has to move a fraction of what the $5 stock must move for you to make money.

This is an understandable viewpoint. But there are a number of reasons why trading penny stocks is almost never in the best interest of the small investor. Before we go into these reasons, let's backtrack a little in case you don't know just what a penny stock is. *Penny stocks* are stocks that are trading under the price of $1. They can range in price from $0.99 to as low as a penny. Many of these stocks are traded on stock exchanges in foreign countries. For example, there are many penny stocks in the Vancouver stock exchange in Canada. Penny stocks also trade in the United States, on exchanges created specifically for low-priced stocks and are often referred to as Over the Counter (OTC) stocks.

Even if you understand what a penny stock is, you still might be confused about why trading them is a bad idea. First of all, trading penny stocks puts you at risk of falling prey to stock scams. If you've ever seen the movie *The Boiler Room*, you might recall how the characters easily tricked unsuspecting investors into buying stock in "dead" companies. Because it is hard to find information on the business of these companies, an individual or a group can issue false information about such stocks. In doing so, they convince small investors to buy those stocks, pumping the price up for themselves. Such types of stock scams, though highly illegal, are more likely to be perpetrated using penny stocks.

The second problem with trading penny stocks is also caused by lack of information. Often the management of these companies has had questionable experience and their products are of questionable quality. In fact, it may be hard to obtain information on exactly who is running the company and what its products are. If you cannot find this type of information on a company, you should not even begin to consider buying the stock. If you cannot figure out who is running a company, or what its business is, it is likely that few other people know or care. Companies like this have little or no chance of success.

Another issue when trading penny stocks pertains to trading foreign stocks in general. If you trade American Depositary Receipts (ADRs), you don't need to worry about this: Normal SEC rules apply to these issues. However, when trading on foreign stock exchanges, strange things can happen. Unfamiliar or unexpected rules may apply, and rules that we take for granted on U.S.-based exchanges may no longer apply. For safety's sake, stick with domestic stocks and ADRs.

TOO MANY CHOICES FOR ONE INVESTOR!

So what happens now? We've given you numerous tools to determine which stocks under $10 are viable. You should apply these tools to a reasonable number of symbols (the more, the better), and come up with a list of about ten stocks that work with the criteria above. But once you've found these symbols, how do you decide which ones to buy?

Your first instinct may be to buy the cheapest ones. But even a complete monkey-brain should be able to tell by now that cheaper is not necessarily better! To determine which stocks you should buy, read Chapter 6 on technical analysis. Although this chapter may be challenging to the new investor, it is a crucial step toward making successful investments. Without technical analysis, you will have no objective system to tell you which stocks to buy and sell. Don't be an ignorant monkey and pick the first ripe bananas you see.

LOW-PRICED MUTUAL FUNDS

Low-priced mutual funds provide a unique advantage to the stock market investor. Because of the turbulent nature of today's financial markets, diversification of portfolio holdings is increasingly important. If you begin investing in stock with even the smallest amount of money, low-priced mutual funds can provide the safety of a diversified portfolio. Of course, some funds will be riskier than others. Some sector-specific funds, such as technology funds, have shown dismal returns over the past few years. Even at low prices, they might not be wise investments in terms of risk. However,

TABLE 5-1. LOW-PRICED MUTUAL FUNDS

Symbol	Fund Name	NAV, 8/30/2001
LEXMX	Pilgrim Precious Metals A	2.97
ATCHX	Amerindo Technology D	5.16
ENSPX	Enterprise Small Company Value A	8.24
MMUBX	MFS Utilities B	9.37
CBBCX	Alliance Growth and Income	3.67
ARFCX	ABN AMRO Real Estate Comm.	10.04
PRLAX	T. Rowe Price Latin America	9.44
ETHSX	Eaton Vance Worldwide Health Science A	10.35

other sector-specific funds, such as gold funds, have shown themselves to be stable investments, even at low prices.

Investing in low-priced mutual funds means that you can buy more shares, with less dollar commitment. Larger funds often have restrictions; they require a large initial investment, which you may not be prepared to make. You may be able to afford only a few shares of a higher-priced fund. Investing in numerous low-priced funds means that you will have limited exposure to any one portion of the market. Also, if you want to try less traditional investment ideas, such as buying foreign stocks or investing in REITs (Real Estate Investment Trusts), you can do so by investing in low-priced mutual funds (see Table 5-1). This way, you don't break the bank and you gain the guidance of a market professional.

SUMMARY

Investing in low-priced stocks may seem appealing to the investor with limited resources. However, there are both positive and negative aspects in taking this approach to investing. Here, we outline some of the methods you can use to find the cheap stocks that have a better chance for making you money:

- Check *trading volume* to make sure that a substantial number of investors and traders are buying and selling the stock.
- Find out what the company does, and who its principals are. This is particularly important in relatively unknown, low-priced stocks, because such stocks are sometimes the target of scams and securities fraud.
- Determine the number of outstanding shares, in order to make sure that the stock has the potential to rise with proper trading volume.

- Research institutional ownership and insider activity. This should give you a feeling for what company executives and professional investors feel about the future of the company.
- Find out if the stock has high short interest. If it does, the stock may be prone to *short-covering rallies*. You can take advantage of such rallies using our timing indicators, which will be discussed in Chapter 6.

Buying and selling low-priced stocks can be a little tricky. Make sure to use limit orders instead of market orders. Although limit orders may cost a few dollars more, they won't give you any unpleasant surprises. Because the market for low-priced stocks is often thin, using market orders can have disastrous consequences.

6

THE TECHNICAL APPROACH TO STOCK MARKET STRATEGIES

"We must use time as a tool, not as a couch."
John Fitzgerald Kennedy

There are several different methodologies that a stock investor can use in the quest for profits.

TIMING INDICATORS, SYSTEMS, AND METHODS

Many investors are uncertain about the difference between a timing indicator, a trading system, a trading method, and a trading technique. The following definitions will help you understand these terms as they are used in stocks. Please read them carefully since they will be used extensively throughout this chapter.

Timing Indicators

A *timing indicator* is also known as a timing signal. Investors use timing signals and indicators as strategies and alerts so they will know when a stock should be bought or sold. The accuracy or effectiveness of a timing signal is a function of the underlying validity of the idea on which the indicator is based. If the timing signal you decide to use is based on a completely arbitrary idea, such as how many times a day you stop at stop lights, your timing signal will be less effective than if it is based on something that has to do with stock price or volume fluctuations.

If my timing indicator is to buy a stock every time it goes down a certain number of points from the previous daily closing price, then the results of what I do will be a function of how well this strategy works. There are literally thousands of ideas on which timing indicators and signals are based. We will be teaching you a number of these so that you can decide which ones you prefer to use in your investment strategy.

Traders and investors use timing indicators in order to increase their probability of success in the stock market. All too often traders use timing indicators that are essentially ineffective. Many timing indicators are about as accurate as a coin toss. In other words, their success is questionable. Most of the timing indicators used yield results that are little better than what might be achieved by guessing. The average investor is unaware of this since most popular books teach timing indicators without giving you an idea or even an estimate of how well they work.

Timing indicators are very useful tools. However, if they are to be used to their fullest potential, they must be integrated into trading systems. The next section discusses the trading systems and their relation to timing indicators.

Trading systems. A *trading system* is so named because it is totally systematic. It contains specific rules that are operationally defined, precise, and capable of being implemented by anyone who is familiar with the rules of the system. A trading system contains rules for market entry, market exit, and risk management.

The rules are designed to cover virtually every possibility and, if implemented in the prescribed fashion, should allow the trader to reproduce historical performance as long as the system was designed to produce realistic results. If used correctly, trading systems should also yield the same results regardless of the trader. If two traders make exactly the same decisions because they are using the same system to make those decisions, their end profits or losses should be the same.

Some investors feel that trading systems are too rigid, or that they do not allow the individual to exercise his or her common sense and/or experience when making investment decisions. This, of course, begs the question as to whether investors have common sense, whether common sense is an asset in the markets, and whether experience is of any value when it comes to trading decisions. All of these issues are matters of opinion and have been hotly debated among professionals for many years.

In the case of the beginning investor, it is better to assume that the system is correct. Unless your system has given you a signal that is an obvious, glaring error, you should follow the indications of your system to a tee. Sticking strictly to the rules of the trading system of your choice is very beneficial, because it allows you to easily identify where the system has failed. When you stray from your system, pinpointing your mistakes becomes harder to do, as you have to review your own thought process. Scrutinizing a mechanical system in which exact results can be reproduced is always easier than scrutinizing your own thoughts and feelings, which are hardly tangible to begin with.

Trading methods.   A *trading method* is a combination of timing signals loosely organized and implemented according to a variety of relatively general rules. The investor determines when to buy and sell based on his or her rules, yet these rules are often neither highly specific, nor are they sufficiently thorough. However, people who use trading methods can make money.

Using a trading method instead of a trading system does mean that a certain amount of subjectivity will enter into your investment decisions. Depending on whether you believe that subjectivity is an asset or a liability in trading, you will find the use of a trading method either desirable or unacceptable. In recent years, trading methods have come to be known as "proprietary trading." In using this approach, the trader uses a trading *method* (as opposed to a trading *system*).

Again, we recommend that you use a trading system as opposed to a trading method. The degree of subjectivity that trading methods allow is not appropriate for beginning investors. Some experts would argue that so much subjectivity in making decisions about investments is not appropriate for anyone. In any case, trading on instinct is always significantly riskier than trading using a system, if for no other reason than the fact that when all is said and done, you may not know where you made your mistakes.

TYPES OF TIMING INDICATORS

Timing indicators are divided into three main categories:

* *Leading indicators are indicators that tend to give you buy or sell signals before a stock makes its turn.*

In a sense they forecast a top or a bottom; however, they do not forecast specific price levels or duration of a move. In theory, there are many supposedly leading indicators; however, in practice there are few that truly lead the markets.

We consider leading indicators to be the most useful for the beginning investor or trader. This is because they allow ample time for you to prepare to make your investment. When applying leading indicators to stocks, remember that your indicator is telling you that a move is going to happen. If you look at your stock charts and expect to see that a move has already begun, you will most likely not see it.

Leading indicators seem to offer the investor the best of all worlds. However, there are drawbacks when using such indicators. One major problem occurs because it is easy to buy a stock too early. Exposure to price fluctuations that occur before the beginning of the indicated up or down trend may cause you to bail out early. If you are only willing to take a certain amount of risk in a particular investment, and have bought early because you are using a leading indicator, you may be stopped out of your trade, and thus lose all potential for profit.

- *Time current indicators tend to turn higher or lower at about the same time that a stock does.*

There are many such indicators. They can be very helpful in making long-term investments, and we consider such indicators practically as useful as leading indicators.

The time current indicator should not expose you to as much of the pre-move price fluctuations as the leading indicator does. However, decisions about buying and selling must be made quickly with time current indicators, as the stock should be making its move at the same time that you take your position.

- *Lagging indicators are those that lag behind stock movements.*

Such indicators are like the tail on a kite; the market moves, and the lagging indicator moves after it. These indicators are also known as *trend-following indicators* since they follow trends and do not attempt to forecast them. Using lagging indicators to make decisions about buying and selling leaves you with a particular disadvantage, because you will be buying and selling after the tops and bottoms of market trends.

Using lagging indicators for the long term is still an effective and acceptable method of investing. If you are positioning yourself for moves that may take a year or a number of years to develop, lagging indicators can help you be confident that you have bought or sold into a real trend. Still, if you are late in taking your position and you enter as the trend is turning in the opposite direction, you may become a victim of the dreaded "whipsaw effect."

By this we mean you will be buying at tops and getting out at bottoms—clearly a losing strategy. Hence, lagging indicators must be chosen carefully as a function of their characteristics, or they must be used in conjunction with other indicators that will mitigate this inherent limitation.

The goal in using a lagging indicator is that the trader or investor will be able to profitably grab a significant portion of a trend before the indicator changes direction again. In strong bull or bear markets, leading indicators do excellent work; however, in sideways markets or markets in transition they tend to lose money and suffer from low accuracy.

Price over Time Equals Timing

While most traders throughout the world use price as the indicator of whether to buy or sell a stock, we believe that the price of a stock is not nearly as important as the *timing* of your transaction. In other words, we feel that the investor need not be as concerned about the price of a stock as much as the timing of market entry and exit. Timing is the all-important variable.

While many traders and investors are good at discerning the trend of a market, their timing is often poor. Although such people may be able to tell you that a stock will move in a given direction, they themselves oftentimes have a hard time profiting from their knowledge since their market entry and exit are timed incorrectly. They may buy too late or too early or they may sell too late or too early. This is very likely due to a lack of experience in using timing when getting in and out of trades.

Price is important to the long-term investor. However, good timing can overcome the importance of price. Investors and traders alike must move with the existing trend rather than against it. After all, prices that are cheap tend to get cheaper while prices that are expensive tend to become more expensive (both up to a point). Trends tend to continue in their current direction. That is, a stock is more likely to continue moving in one direction (up or down), rather than reverse that movement.

Opinions as to the importance of both price and timing vary markedly. In reality, an investment and/or trading approach that combines both elements is likely to be more productive and profitable in the long run than a one-sided approach. The coming together of time and price is very important. The investor who can understand and use both price and time effectively is likely to be consistently profitable.

The concept of time and price confluence, when used as a trading system, is a significant and effective approach for making money. While the concept is valid, putting it into practice is a different issue entirely.

Numerous systems and methods have been developed for the sole purpose
of putting this concept into practice.

Someone who buys at support as prices decline in an existing uptrend,
is attempting to harness the power of this approach. The same is true when
one sells short at resistance. In other words, the investor is attempting to
combine price with time by selling at a given price after seeing the market
rally or buying at support when a market declines. Being able to discern
the trend and the price at which to take a position is a powerful tool that
should be mastered, or at least understood, by even the smallest investor.

In order to know exactly when to buy and sell, you will need to be able
to define the following variables:

- *Trend.* What is the current trend? Is the trend up, down, or sideways?
  How "strong" is the trend? Is there a way to quantify the trend? What
  is the "quality" of the trend? Is the market moving sharply higher
  with considerable rapidity and magnitude or is the trend slow and
  steady?

- *Support.* If the trend is up, is there a way to determine where a stock
  should stop its decline when it goes down (temporarily) during a pervasive uptrend? Can a specific price be determined and, if so, how?

- *Resistance.* If the trend is down, is there a way to determine where a
  stock should stop its rally when it goes up (temporarily) during a pervasive downtrend? Can a specific price be determined and, if so,
  how?

The fact is that all three can be ascertained with relative ease. For the time
being, suffice it to say that specific methods for doing so will be presented.
Our intent at this juncture is simply to introduce you to the concept. Here,
then, are some methods for determining trends and/or entry/exit points. In
each case we will explain the method as well as its assets, liabilities, and variations. An example of each technique will be provided in chart form.

There are numerous books on technical analysis that can explain these
approaches in considerable detail. The explanations offered herein are necessarily cursory and are provided only as a general background to the systems and methods we will discuss in later chapters.

AN EXAMINATION OF BASIC TIMING INDICATORS

Given the plethora of trading systems, timing indicators, and methods available to the trader, it is reasonable to expect that most readers will be overwhelmed by the number of choices. Often the amount of available information
in texts or online is insufficient to help you make a decision.

In the long run you are left to make decisions on your own. And, all too often, these decisions cannot be made without reference to historical performance. As you can imagine, this poses a formidable challenge to the newcomer. But this is no surprise. All too often information about what works or what doesn't work in the markets is not available to the public in spite of all the books, seminars, and courses that are available.

Hopefully, the explanations that follow will help elucidate for you the indicators and methods that we feel work best and under what circumstances. We will give you an evaluation of their assets and liabilities, all based on our experience in the stock and commodity markets.

Moving Average Indicators (MAs): Traditional and Advanced

Whether you use one, two, or many MAs, the concepts and applications are essentially similar. Either the market price must close above or below its MAs to signal a buy or a sell, or the MAs themselves must change their relationship to one another in order to signal a trade. Richard Donchian popularized this approach in the 1950s although it was probably being used well before then.

In the typical MA-based system, signals are generated in either of several ways:

- Price closes above or below its MA. Closing above the MA is considered a buy signal whereas closing below the MA is considered a sell signal.
- In the case of multiple MAs, the approach signals buy or sell signals when the various lengths of MAs cross one another.
- In the case of MAs of closing/opening, or high or low prices, signals are generated when crossovers of the MAs occur as defined by the theory or method.

Assets.   Traditional MA indicators tend to do extremely well in major trends. They can make you a lot of money after a major trend has started if you are able to hold on to your position. MAs are lagging indicators since they give signals *after* a market has made its turn. There are numerous variations on the theme of the MA—some more effective and responsive than others. Most computer trading systems allow you to use different mathematical formulations of the MA (that is, weighted, exponential, smoothed, displaced, centered, and so on).

Figure 6-1 shows a stock chart with various moving averages plotted against it. Note the rather large differences. MAs can also be used to determine trend. In the traditional approach, price above its MA indicates an

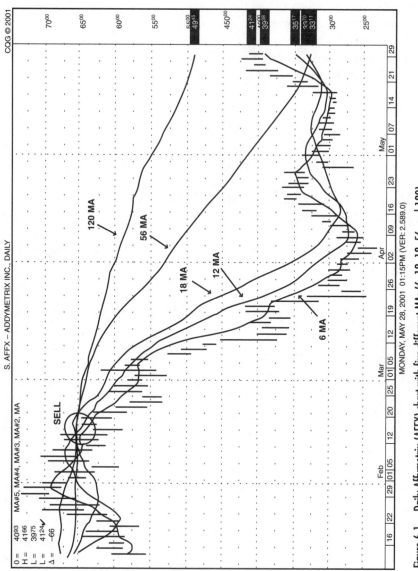

Figure 6-1. Daily Affymetrix (AFFX) chart with five different MAs (6, 12, 18, 56, and 120).

uptrend, whereas price below its MA indicates a downtrend. In the example provided (Figure 6-1) the stock is in a downtrend after having crossed below its MA. It remains in an uptrend. Note that in February, the stock was in a downtrend after falling below all of its moving averages. One thing you will observe, without a doubt, is that moving averages are lagging indicators, as previously stated. Therefore, if you use moving averages in the traditional sense, be prepared to get in and out after a stock has already made its high or low. At times, late entry and/or exit can be very costly.

Liabilities.   These indicators tend to give many false (that is, losing) signals. They will often get you into a move well after it has started, and when a change in trend occurs, they will often get you out after you have given back a considerable amount of your profit. Such moving averages tend to be inaccurate and often have considerable drawdown as well as numerous consecutive losing trades.

Solutions.   Some of the problems with moving averages can be minimized as follows:

- Use a weighted, exponential, smoothed, or displaced MA.
- Use a different MA length to exit a trade than you use to enter a trade.
- Use different MA lengths for buy signals and sell signals.
- Use another indicator to confirm or negate an MA.
- Or, use an adaptive MA (AMA). A more recent addition to the MA arsenal, the AMA tends to be more responsive to price changes by using several variables. To accomplish this, the AMA uses an efficiency ratio (ER) and smoothing constant.

Variations on the Theme of Moving Averages
There are many variations on the theme of moving averages. These include MA-based oscillators such as the MACD, the MA Channel, and various high and/or low MA combinations.

Assets.   These variations on the MA tend to be more accurate and more sensitive than simple MA combinations of the closing price. The MACD was specifically designed for S&P trading by Gerald Appel while the Moving Average Channel (MAC) is our own creation. Figure 6-2 shows a daily chart (also AFFX as in Figure 6-1) with the MACD. Buy-and-sell signals on the MACD are generated when the two MACD lines cross one another.

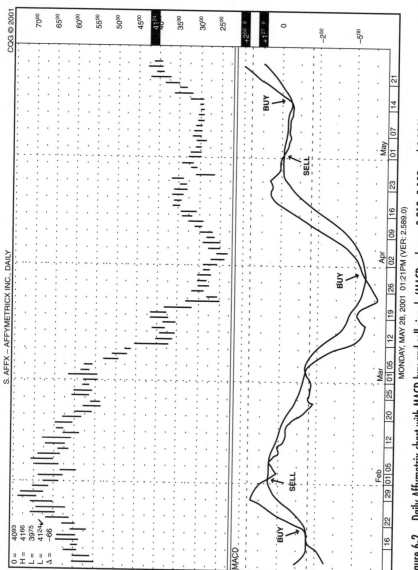

Figure 6-2. Daily Affymetrix chart with MACD buy-and-sell signals (MACD values = 0.218, 0.108, and 0.199).

The MAC can also be used to determine concise support and resistance levels. It will be discussed in considerable detail as a trading method in Chapter 8.

Liabilities.   There is a tendency, as with many MA-based systems, to give back too much profit once a change in trend has developed. This is true of all lagging indicators.

Solutions.   Here are some suggestions as to how one might overcome the limitations of MA-based indicators:

- Use a shorter combination of MA lengths for exit. Hence, exit will be triggered before the MAs indicate a reversal in trend.
- Use another indicator to confirm the MA signals.
- Use another indicator that is not MA-based for exiting positions.
- Develop a trailing stop-loss plan that will enhance exit while not significantly diminishing system accuracy.

Stochastics (SI) and the Relative Strength Index (RSI)

Dr. George Lane popularized the Stochastic Indicator (SI) and its use. The Relative Strength Index (RSI) is very similar to the SI. The difference is that SI has two values; RSI has only one. Computing a moving average of the first SI value derives the second SI value. Both indicators are often used to indicate theoretically "overbought" or "oversold" conditions. They may both be used as timing indicators as well as indicators of so-called overbought and oversold conditions.

Figure 6-3 shows the daily AT&T (T) chart with a stochastic and an RSI. There are various methods and interpretations of the SI and RSI. SI signals are shown on the chart (Figure 6-3). Note that there are many different methods of using RSI and SI for the purpose of finding trends, buy signals, and sell signals.

Those included on Figure 6-3 are not being touted as the best. They are merely included as examples for informational and introductory purposes. As you can see, both indicators can generate numerous signals. The number of signals can be adjusted by changing the length of the indicators.

Assets.   Both the RSI and SI have considerable sex appeal. By this, we mean they look good on a chart. They tend to identify tops and bottoms quite well. They are also useful in timing provided one uses the appropriate crossover areas for timing trades.

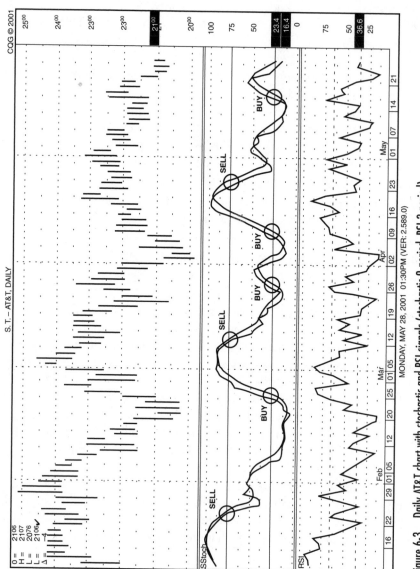

Figure 6-3. Daily AT&T chart with stochastic and RSI signals (stochastic 9-period, RSI 3-period).

Liabilities.   The concepts of "overbought" and "oversold" are not useful and often misleading. Frequently markets that are overbought continue to go considerably higher while markets that are oversold continue to go considerably lower.

Solutions

- Don't use the SI and RSI for determining overbought or oversold conditions. Use these indicators as timing methods when the readings cross above or below certain values. You might also consider the use of RSI and SI with other timing indicators.
- Use the SI "POP" method that may be helpful in trading moves that occur in overbought and oversold territory.
- Another method of using the RSI and SI is to exit trades using a shorter SI or RSI indicator length than was used for entry.

Chart Patterns and Formations

These methods are based on the traditional techniques as proposed by Edwards and Magee as well as other tools such as those developed by W. D. Gann, George Bayer, and R. N. Elliott. There are many different chart formations and various outcomes possible for each. They require a good deal of study and are, at times, quite intricate as well as subjective. The commodity trading literature is rich with methods and systems based on these patterns.

Assets

- *These methods are highly visual.* In other words, you can draw lines on a piece of paper, or you can examine patterns visually, and see what should be done.
- *The methods don't necessarily require a computer.*
- *They can easily be learned by almost anyone.* Frequently the prescribed actions are specific once you have completed the necessary interpretation of the chart patterns.
- *The methods are usually quite logical.* Hence, they have a good deal of face validity.

Liabilities

- In most cases these methods are highly subjective and difficult to test for accuracy.
- The Gann and Elliott methods have been known and used by traders for many years; however, there is considerable disagreement, even among experts, as to what patterns exist at any given point in time and, in fact, how these patterns should be traded.

Solutions. A possible solution would be to use the methods in conjunction with other timing that is more objective and operational.

Parabolic

This is a method that is based on a mathematical formula derived from the parabolic curve. It provides the trader with two values each day, a "sell number" and a "buy number." These serve as sell stops and buy stops. Penetration of the buy number means to go long and close out the short, while penetration of the sell number means to close out long and go short.

Figure 6-4 shows the daily Priceline.com (PCLN) chart with the parabolic indicator. As you can see, there were two signals.

Assets

• The parabolic indicator is totally objective. It can be used as a mechanical trading system with risk management methods.

• It provides a buy and sell stop daily and is therefore capable of changing orientation from long to short very quickly.

Liabilities

• Parabolic can get "whipsawed" badly in sideways or highly volatile markets.

• Parabolic can catch some very large moves; however, it has many of the same limitations that are inherent in the use of traditional moving averages.

Solutions

• Use parabolic with other indicators that are not necessarily based on price, that is, volume and/or open interest.

• Use shorter-term time frames for exiting parabolic trades.

• Since parabolic in its pure form is an "always in the market" system, you may be able to adapt it by specifying certain conditions in which it goes into a neutral state (in other words, no position).

Directional Movement Indicator (DMI) and
Average Directional Movement Indicator (ADX)

These are unique indicators based on reasonable solid theories about market movement. They are calculated with relative ease and may be used either objectively as part of a trading system, or as trend and market strength indicators.

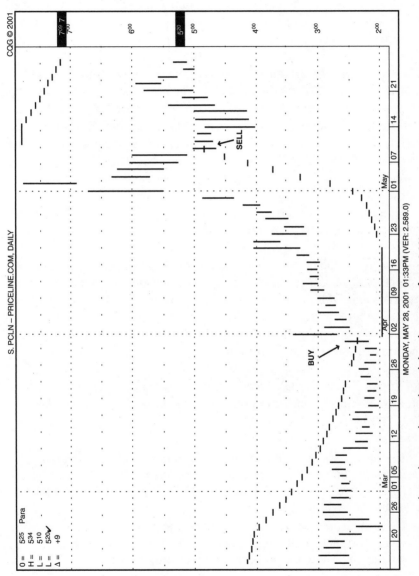

Figure 6-4. Daily Priceline.com chart with parabolic indicator (step factor 0.02).

69

DMI—Directional Movement Indicator.   The Directional Movement Indicator (DMI) was developed by Wells Wilder. The indicator is used to determine if a stock is "trending" or "not trending." DMI has three values: the **+DI**, the **-DI**, and the **ADX**, which we will discuss next. Wilder suggests that you buy when the +DI crosses above the -DI. He suggests short sales when the +DI crosses below the -DI. ADX is a smoothed version of the directional movement.

ADX—Average Directional Movement Index (a Derivative of DMI). ADX is a derivative of the directional movement indicator. It measures the *strength* of a market trend, not its direction. The higher the ADX, the more "directional" the market. The lower the ADX, the less "directional" the market. ADX does not measure whether a stock is rising or falling. The Overbought/Oversold (OB/OS) parameter sets boundaries on the strength or weakness of the *trend*, rather than on the strength or weakness of the *stock itself.*[1]

Figure 6-5 shows an application of the ADX, on a daily Brocade Communications (BRCD) chart.

Assets.   These methods are not based on effete concepts or market myths. They are well worth investigating for development into trading systems. The ADX and DMI are not used by many traders. Their main focus is on the strength of a trend and, as a result, is somewhat different in its approach. Both timing methods can be very helpful when used in conjunction with other timing indicators.

Liabilities.   ADX and DMI tend to lag somewhat behind market tops and bottoms. As a result, they can give signals that may be somewhat late.

Solutions
- *Use these indicators in conjunction with other indicators that are based on different theoretical understandings of the markets.* The DMI difference is a variation on the DMI. It is the indicator I recommend for DMI analysis.
- *Use a derivative of the DMI or ADX as part of your method.* In other words, compute a moving average of the ADX or the DMI and use the moving average to develop more accurate timing.

---

[1] For more about the ADM Index, see *Computer Analysis of the Futures Markets* by Charles LeBeau and David W. Lucas, or *New Concepts in Technical Trading Systems* by Welles Wilder, Trend Research, Greensboro, NC, 1978.

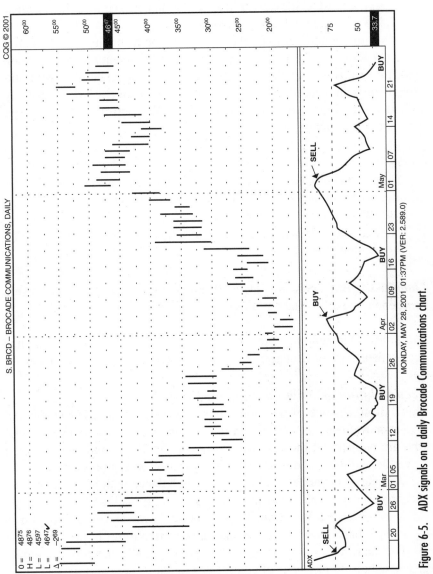

Figure 6-5. ADX signals on a daily Brocade Communications chart.

71

Momentum and/or Rate of Change (ROC)

These indicators are actually one and the same in the final analysis. Although they are derived using different mathematical operations, their output is the same in terms of highs, lows, and trends. I believe that both momentum and ROC have been ignored and underrated as trading indicators and as valid inputs for trading systems.

When momentum crosses above its zero line from a negative reading, a stock is considered to be in a bull trend. When momentum crosses below zero from a positive reading, the stock is considered to be in a bull trend. Momentum can be used in any time frame (that is, daily, intraday, weekly, and so forth). Figure 6-6 illustrates one application of momentum, yet there are many more.

Assets

• These indicators are very adaptable. They can be used not only as indicators but they can also be developed into specific trading systems with risk management.

• They can be used with other indicators such as a moving average of the momentum.

Liabilities.   Both indicators lag market turns to a given extent. As a result, they tend to be a little late at tops and bottoms.

Solutions.   Momentum and rate of change indicators can be plotted against their own moving averages in order to reduce the time lag of signals.

Accumulation Distribution and Its Derivative

This indicator is one of the more important ones for the stock trader. All market movements are a function of the ongoing struggle between those who are bullish and those who are bearish. While the bulls have buying power behind them, the bears have the power of selling pressure.

As long as buyers and sellers remain in balance with no group having clear control, prices remain in limbo, oscillating back and forth but not exhibiting any clear direction. At some point, however, one group gains a clear upper hand, and the trend makes a concerted move in that direction.

For many years, traders have attempted to find a method that would give insight as to the focus of control in a market. Clearly, if we can know which group is in "control," we can either buy or sell accordingly with a relatively high degree of probability that we will be right.

By "control" I mean the "balance of power." The question as to whether the bulls or the bears are "in control" of a market is an important

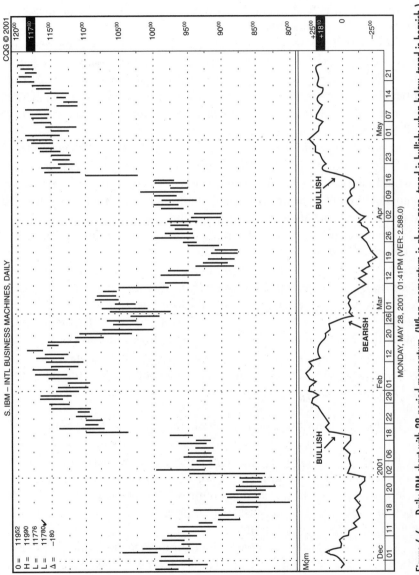

Figure 6-6. Daily IBM chart with 28-period momentum. (When momentum is above zero, trend is bullish; when below, trend is bearish.)

73

one, particularly for the day trader. If we know that the bulls are in control
of a market then we will do well to buy on declines, knowing that the market is likely to recover from its drop. Buying on declines is not a simple
matter. There are specific points at which we will want to buy on declines
in a market that is in firm control of the bulls. These will be delineated in
our discussion of support and resistance.

In a market that is controlled by the bears, rallies will be relatively
short lived as sellers overpower buyers and the market returns to its declining trend. By *control* we do not mean to imply that there is an actual group
of buyers or sellers who are conspiring to control the direction of a market.
By control we mean essentially "balance of power." In such a market we
will want to be sellers at resistance.

In a perfect world we would like to see markets follow our model or
theory as closely as possible. While this would simplify our task as traders,
it would likely mean an end to free markets since virtually every market
trend and trend change would be predictable and there would, therefore, be
no markets. Yet, we know that this is not the case.

Given the imperfect state of affairs in the stock and futures markets, it
would be advantageous to have available to us any indicators or systems
that will reveal the balance of power in a given market. For the stock trader, such a method would likely prove very profitable if correctly employed.

How could such a method work and what measure of buying or selling power can we use to assist in our task as day traders? Theoretically, as
a stock that has been in a bull trend begins to move sideways or makes an
abrupt top, a change of control is taking place as the bears gain the upper
hand over the bulls. One interpretation is that selling pressure outweighs
buying power. Prices begin to turn lower, yet there is likely advance indication that this is about to happen.

During and prior to a sideways phase, the bears are "distributing" contracts to the bulls. The bulls eventually reach a point where their cumula-
tive buying can no longer sustain an uptrend, and the market drops as the
bears continue their selling. Hence, we call this phase *distribution*. Note
the left-hand portion of the chart in Figure 6-7, using the accumulation-distribution indicator. It shows distribution prior to a large decline followed
by a lengthy period of accumulation.

At a market bottom the reverse holds true. Accumulation takes place
as bulls gain the upper hand, overpowering selling by the bears. In theory,
buying power outweighs the selling pressure. There is cumulatively more
buying than selling. Eventually the balance is overcome as buying demand
outpaces the supply of selling and the market surges higher. The bulls gain
firm control, and prices move higher.

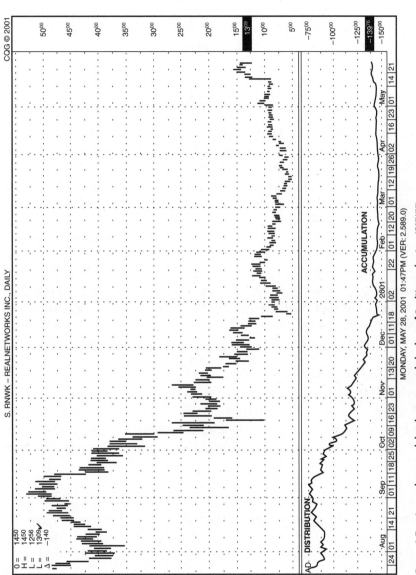

Figure 6-7. Accumulation and distribution on a daily chart of RealNetworks, Inc. (RNWK).

75

Theoretically, the bulls are slowly but surely gaining control of the market during the bottoming or "accumulation" phase. Figure 6-8 illustrates both conditions using the accumulation-distribution indicator in Cisco Systems (CSCO).

In spite of our wonderful theories and their face validity, stocks do not always conform to their ideal situations. At times a stock will change trend almost immediately and seemingly without notice. Purists will argue that in such cases markets do give advance warnings but that the signs are subtle. We agree. But note that if the signs cannot be found, then the theory, no matter how seemingly valid, will not help us.

The Advance/Decline Indicator

What we have just described for you is the theory of accumulation and distribution. The theory is simple, reasonable, logical, and easy to understand. The difficult part is finding methods, indicators, and/or technical trading systems that will allow traders to take advantage of the hypothetical constructs both on a longer-term and day-trade basis.

One such indicator is the Advance/Decline (A/D) oscillator originally developed by Larry Williams and James J. Waters in 1972. Their article entitled "Measuring Market Momentum" appeared in the October 1972 issue of *Commodities Magazine*. It introduced their A/D oscillator.

The purpose of the oscillator was to detect changes in the balance of power from buyers to sellers and vice versa. Calculation of the A/D oscillator is a relatively simple matter. A thorough explanation and critical evaluation of the A/D oscillator can be found in *The New Commodity Trading Systems and Methods*.[2]

The A/D oscillator is also available in preprogrammed form on many of the popular software analysis systems such as Commodity Quote Graphics (CQG) and TradeStation. The formula for calculating A/D can be obtained either in the original Williams' and Waters' article or the Kaufman book (cited above).

Using the A/D Oscillator

There are several potential applications of the A/D oscillator for position and day trading. They range from the artistic and interpretive to the mechanical and objective. While our application may not be as scientific as one would like, our efforts are in the correct direction. One method we have worked with extensively is to buy and sell based on when the A/D

[2] Kaufman, Perry, *The New Commodity Trading Systems and Methods*, NY: John Wiley & Sons, 1987, pp. 102–106.

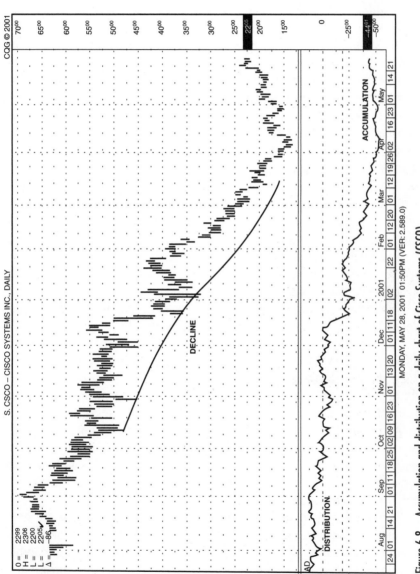

Figure 6-8. Accumulation and distribution on a daily chart of Cisco Systems (CSCO).

77

oscillator crosses above and below the zero line. See Figure 6-9 for an example of what can happen when A/D falls below zero.

All too often a stock will move higher and higher while the A/D is in negative ground and vice versa. Such situations not only confuse the trader into thinking that the theory is incorrect but they are also costly since they produce losses.

Yet another limitation of the A/D and, indeed, of all oscillators, is that they can frequently move back and forth above and below the zero line numerous times before a sustained trend emerges. Traders who buy and sell on such frequent crosses above and below the zero line will suffer numerous repeated losses, not to mention the cost of commissions and slippage. But there's a way to overcome this serious limitation.

The Advance/Decline Derivative (ADD)

The word *derivative* means exactly what it says. It is a value that is derived by a mathematical manipulation of another value. In other words, the first derivative of any number is a new number that is derived from the initial number. If, for example, I have a 24-period moving average as my original value and then I calculate a 20-day moving average of the 24-period moving average, then the 20-day moving average is the first derivative of the 24-period moving average.

If I calculate a moving average of the A/D oscillator, then the moving average I calculate is termed the first derivative of the A/D since it is derived from the A/D value. One purpose of calculating a derivative is to smooth the values of the original data. Our purpose is to do this as well as to use the derivative value and the A/D value for generating signals that will help overcome the limitations of the A/D oscillator when used alone (as mentioned earlier).

As presented here, the ADD method is objective but not entirely systematic. In order to use it as a system you will need to add a risk management stop-loss and/or a trailing stop-loss (if you prefer). This will make the method useful as a system. Naturally, you will want to trade the ADD in active and volatile markets only.

The ADD method also has potential for use in day trading. The ADD is a highly versatile indicator lending itself for use in all time frames. Traders interested in using this approach are encouraged to research it more thoroughly as a trading system with risk management rules before using it extensively for day trading. As an example of how the ADD generates signals, see Figures 6-10 and 6-11. Each shows the ADD with signals on stock charts of Amazon.com.

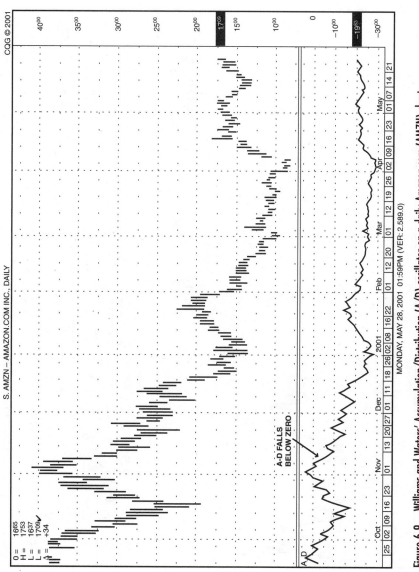

Figure 6-9. Williams and Waters' Accumulation/Distribution (A/D) oscillator on a daily Amazon.com (AMZN) chart.

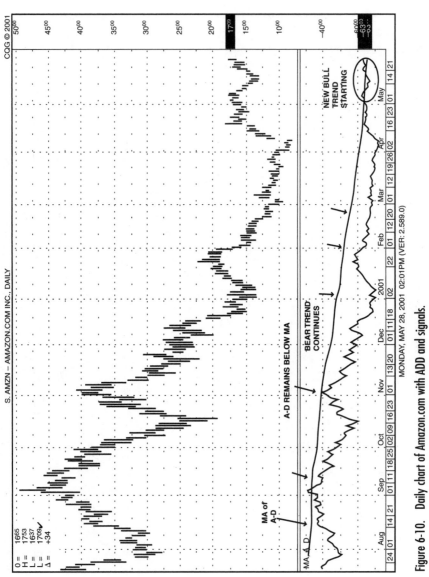

Figure 6-10. Daily chart of Amazon.com with ADD and signals.

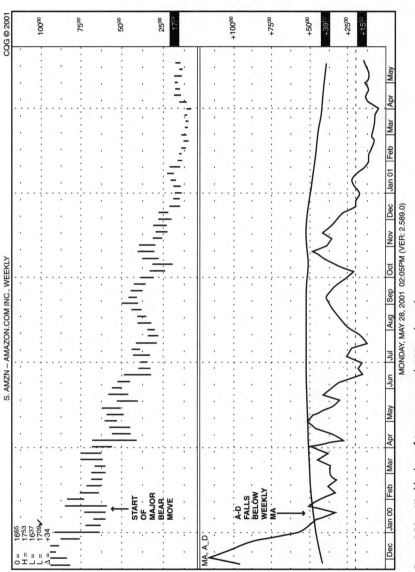

Figure 6-11. Weekly chart of Amazon.com with ADD and signals.

Other Technical Indicators

Perhaps you did not find your favorite indicators included in the section above. Know that what you just read is intended to serve as a general introduction. There is much more technical information to follow. If we consider all of the timing indicators that have been developed over the years, as well as the many variations on the theme of these signals, there are literally thousands of possibilities that confront the day trader.

While it's true that the vast majority of these indicators are either useless or specious, there are some that can prove very valuable to the stock day trader. Our goal is to alert you to those, which we believe to be effective and, moreover, to show how they can be used. In the chapters that follow we will employ some of the indicators discussed above as the core of specific trading systems and methods. We hope these will assist you in your goal of day trading for profits.

ELEMENTS OF AN EFFECTIVE STOCK TRADING SYSTEM

This is the highest and most specific level of trading approaches. As noted in my previous discussion on trading systems, a trading system provides features that make it preferable to all other methods of trading. An effective system will tell you which stock to trade, when to buy, when to sell, how much to risk, and much more. While some traders prefer to use indicators and methods as opposed to systems, we believe that using a system will give you the greatest odds of success.

Here are the essential elements that an effective stock day-trading system must contain (as a point of information, these factors also apply to trading systems that seek to capture longer-term moves as well):

- It contains purely objective rules for market entry and exit.
- It contains risk management rules such as stop-loss and trailing stop-loss.
- It tells you which stocks to trade, and when to trade them.
- It can be back-tested to test its validity using the indicated rules.
- Its signals are not subject to interpretations—they are operational, totally objective, specific, and repeatable.
- Historical back-test performance provides key statistics and hypothetical results.
- Different traders should be able to get exactly the same signals using similar inputs.

There are other fine details that characterize a trading system; however, those indicated above are the most important. Clearly the good news about trading systems is that they can be implemented specifically and without interpretation. The bad news for many stock day traders is that they are unable to follow a trading system due to their lack of discipline.

They would much rather wallow in subjective indicators than have the self-confidence and self-discipline to trade a mechanical system. This book will present several day-trading systems for stocks; yet no matter how good they may look on paper or in back-testing, they will prove totally useless or even unprofitable to the trader who lacks discipline and consistency.

SUPPORT AND RESISTANCE CONCEPTS

Perhaps the single most valuable tool that a day trader can possess is the ability to determine support and resistance. My working definition of *support* as it applies to trading is as follows: the price level at which a market is expected to halt its declining trend and from which prices are expected to move higher at best or sideways at worst.

As you can see, this is a purely pragmatic definition. It is tailor-made to the task at hand. But we hasten to add here that support, in and of itself, is not particularly useful unless it is combined with knowledge of the existing trend. In an uptrend, the support level or area of a stock is likely to halt a short-term decline within the existing trend. Market technicians have developed numerous ways in which to determine support. The most common of these is to draw support trend lines under the price of a stock. While this can be effective, it is too subjective and often fails to provide sufficient information.

Other methods for determining support are based on percentage retracements, moving averages, previous highs and lows, reversal levels, waves, angles, Fibonacci numbers, market geometry, and a host of other methods, some seemingly logical and others that smack of superstition or magic.

We will avoid most of the common and popular methods in favor of several that I have developed over the past thirty years, which I believe to be highly effective. However, we do not expect you to merely take my word as gospel. We suggest that you critically evaluate my methods by watching them and seeing for yourself whether they can be helpful to you in your trading.

As an example of support, consider Figure 6-12. This figure shows a daily chart of Corr Therapeutics (CORR) with my calculated support line. You will notice how the price of this stock continues to "bounce" off support. This is the ideal way in which a valid support line should work in an uptrend.

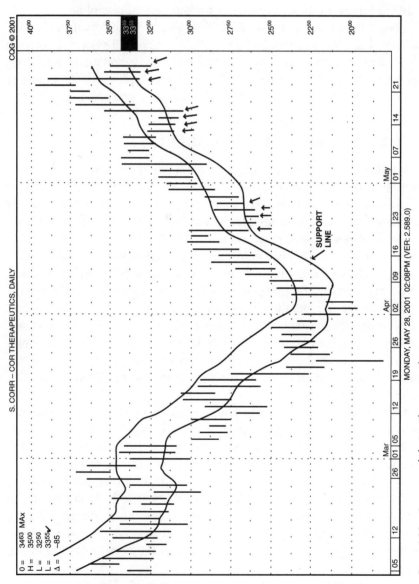

Figure 6-12. Support on daily Corr Therapeutics chart.

Conversely, resistance is an important consideration in a downtrending market. *Resistance* is defined as follows for our purposes: *the price level at which a market is expected to halt its upward trend and from which prices are expected to move lower at worst or sideways at best.*

As in the case of support, there are literally hundreds of ways for determining resistance that traders have developed. The vast majority of them are ineffective. Yet we must remember that the use of resistance (and support) is typically part of a trading method and not always systematic. Hence, the availability to make money using resistance and support is, to a great extent, a function of the trader's skill level and experience. Figure 6-13 shows an example of how prices act when they hit resistance in a downtrend.

THE VALUE OF DAY TRADING WITH SUPPORT AND RESISTANCE

Support and resistance are valuable tools for the day trader. Knowing support and resistance levels, as well as the existing trend, can allow the day trader to accomplish the following goals:

- To buy, at or near support, in an uptrending market and to take profit either at a predetermined objective or at resistance
- To sell short, at or near resistance, in a downtrending market and to take profit either at a predetermined objective or at support
- To avoid markets that are either trendless or whose trading range is insufficient to allow reasonable intra-day price movement
- To buy a market when it overcomes resistance and, therefore, to go for a larger profit inasmuch as the uptrend is likely to remain strong since resistance has been overcome
- To sell a market when it falls below support and, therefore, to go for a larger profit since the downtrend is likely to remain strong now that support has been penetrated

In order to achieve these goals the trader will need to know, as precisely as possible, and with as much accuracy as possible the current trend, the current support level, the current resistance level, and when a change in trend has taken place.

While these seem simple enough, they are lofty goals, not easily attained unless one uses the right methods. A good portion of what follows in this book will address the germane issues I have just cited.

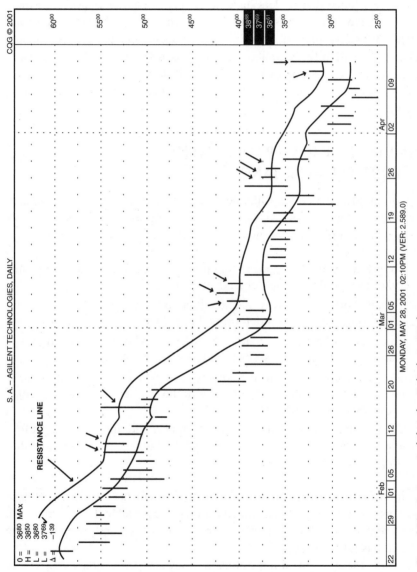

Figure 6-13. Resistance in daily Agilent Technologies (A) chart.

SUMMARY

This chapter examined, in overview, a number of essential concepts in the area of technical analysis and day trading. Key concepts were defined. Numerous timing indicators were introduced. Later chapters will expand on the indicators discussed in this chapter.

C H A P T E R

7

DOLLAR COST AVERAGING: AN OVERVIEW

"Patience, n. A minor form of despair, disguised as a virtue."

Ambrose Bierce

Another stock trading method that works well is called *dollar cost averaging*, or DCA. As with all investing and trading methods, it has its good, bad, and ugly sides. If you can take advantage of the good while minimizing the bad and avoiding the ugly, you'll come out way ahead in the long run. The key words here are "in the long run." After we've explained the method to you, you'll understand clearly why we emphasize "in the long run."

ABOUT DCA

Other terms for DCA are "scale trading" and "spaced repetition." DCA is about optimism. We say that because DCA is exactly what the name implies. Simply stated, you buy stocks on a regular basis as determined either by price, time, investment amount, or a combination of the above. In effect, you average your cost over time.

If you have picked good stocks (that is, stocks that don't go bankrupt or sit at the same price for many years) then, in the long run, you can do extremely well. There are many sources of information on this approach. We'd like to think that what follows in this chapter is more detailed, more comprehensive, and much more effective than what other books have told you.

We believe that DCA can be an excellent tool if you modify the "old rules." The standard rules that have been followed and believed and touted by brokers and market advisers for many years don't work as well as the claims. We think our approach to DCA is more sensible, more manageable, and more rational given market conditions since the early 1980s. Let's take a look at the specifics of this approach in order to get a good handle on what it's all about.

HOW DOLLAR COST AVERAGING WORKS

DCA is based on the following ideas:

- You buy stocks and/or mutual funds at regular time intervals.
- You are in for the longer term.
- You buy a fixed dollar amount (or you can add to the amount).
- You buy only when prices are below a certain point.
- You take profits when prices rise above a certain level, or you use a stop-loss.

The best way to illustrate this approach is by an example. You have been watching the stock of XYZ Company. It has been a stable stock for many years. In fact, you have looked at the long-term price chart and made the astute observation that XYZ has frequently gone down to the $6 to $8 area and then back to about $24 with fairly good consistency over the last twenty-five years. You begin a DCA program as follows:

- You have about $150 to invest each month.

- As long as XYZ is historically high in price, you take no action. This is not a hard and fast rule. You could begin at any time regardless of price but you will make more money if you begin when prices are relatively low based on historical patterns.

- Because you want to make the most amount of money possible, you begin your program when XYZ drops in price.

- The specific approach to DCA, along with a detailed example, is discussed in Chapter 10.

SUMMARY

The dollar cost averaging (DCA) approach is a very effective method of investing if you are willing to wait a long time. By averaging your cost in a given stock or stocks, you eventually achieve a low price, and when the stock begins to move up you can make a great deal of money. The best time to use a DCA is when stocks have been declining. It is best to buy well-established, quality stocks in a DCA program. Any of the traditional blue chip stocks (that is, stocks that make up the Dow Jones Industrial Average) or other well-known stocks with earnings and a long history of profitability are excellent candidates for this approach.

C H A P T E R 8

SUPPORT AND RESISTANCE: THE MAC

"The trend is your friend to the end."
Larry R. Williams

Perhaps two of the oldest, most well-known, and most time-tested ideas in stock (and futures) trading are support and resistance. As the names imply, support and resistance are specific price areas or price levels that either support prices on declines in uptrends or that resist prices on rallies in downtrends. In an uptrend, short-term and day traders will attempt to buy at support or at levels of support. In a downtrend, short-term and day traders will attempt to sell at resistance levels or in resistance areas.

The concept makes a great deal of sense. No matter how complex or intricate methods of market analysis and trading systems have become through the years, ideas of support and resistance have been pervasive and enduring. The only problem is that these ideas require a reasonably objective method for determining support and resistance in order that trades may be entered based on them. If support and resistance cannot be determined, then you cannot define concise levels or areas in which to establish and/or exit positions. Therefore, it behooves traders as well as investors to develop effective strategies and technical methodologies for calculating or determining support and resistance levels.

For many years such levels have been determined using a wide range of tools such as support and resistance trend lines, various chart formations, Gann angles, ratio retracements, Fibonnaci numbers, the golden mean constant, point and figure charter, and others too numerous to mention. Many arcane methods have been employed in efforts to determine support and resistance, some successful at times, others successful frequently, and all too many unsuccessful a vast majority of the time.

Regardless of the fads in market timing methods that have occurred in the futures markets since the 1950s, ideas of support and resistance have endured, and with good reason. The simple fact of the matter is that if calculated correctly, they work. It is the purpose of this chapter to explain and illustrate for you my ideas of support and resistance, in particular as they pertain to stock trading and investing.

The stock trader is in an advantageous position when it comes to the use of support and resistance levels, inasmuch as stock trends tend to be fairly stable once they have started to move in a particular direction. Frequently, trends will continue for a long period of time. During the course of the trend, the stock trader will have numerous opportunities to either buy at technical support in an uptrend or for the more adventurous, to go short at technical resistance in a downtrend. In order to accomplish this goal successfully, the following information must be gleaned:

- Is the trend up or down? Is there an objective way by which the trend can be determined specifically?
- If the trend is up, is there an objective way to determine where and when one should buy at support?
- If the trend is down, is there an objective way to determine when and where one should sell at resistance?

If we can answer the above questions specifically, then we have achieved the admirable goal of trading with the trend.

DETERMINING SUPPORT AND RESISTANCE

Determining support and resistance levels is a relatively simple matter. Although there have been many attempts through the years to develop methods that will define support and resistance levels as precisely as possible, few have been able to achieve this lofty goal. In fact, we wouldn't be surprised if there are as many traders as there are techniques that purport to project support and resistance. We have developed a technique, called the moving average channel (MAC), which has shown itself to be extremely valuable and highly specific. Although this technique was originally developed for use in long-term trading, we have found it to be applicable to short-term and day trading as well.

THE MOVING AVERAGE CHANNEL

Borrowing from concepts originally introduced in the 1950s by Richard Donchian, we departed from the traditional use of moving averages. We conducted intensive research on moving average channels (MACs), which consisted of a moving average of high prices and a moving average of low prices. Rather than focus on closing prices, we felt that support and resistance should be determined using high and low prices, since high and low prices are specifically geared to ideas of support and resistance.

Typically, resistance tends to be found near previous highs, and support tends to be found near previous lows. It therefore occurred to us that rather than examine moving averages of closing prices for support or resistance, it might be better to use moving averages of lows and highs to determine support and resistance, respectively. What we discovered took us several years to fully believe and several more to implement.

Our technique uses a moving average of the high and a moving average of the low in conjunction, which form a moving average channel that is used for determining support and resistance. Figure 8-1 illustrates the MAC used on a daily price chart. The chart consists of a 10-day moving average of the daily highs and an 8-day moving average of the daily lows for this stock. These two values, 10-high and 8-low, do not change from stock to stock.

In other words, no matter what stock we are tracking, we use a 10-day moving average of its highs and an 8-day moving average of its lows. The channel, which consists of the values so derived, gives us all of the information we need in order to make a judgment about the trend, support, and resistance for each stock we are following.

As you can see, the channel has some distinct characteristics. They are summarized as follows:

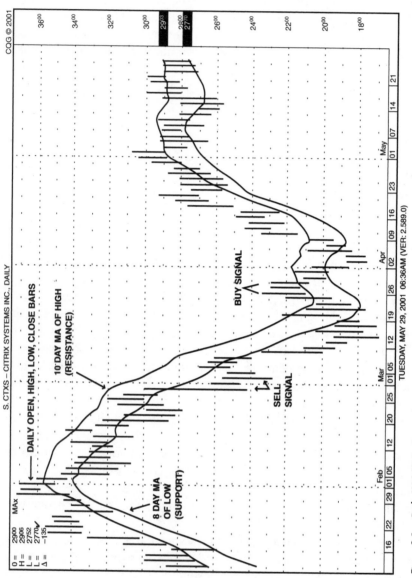

Figure 8-1. Daily MAC (Citrix Systems).

1.

When the trend of prices is up, the MAC tends to act as support. In other words, as price declines to the lower portion of the channel, the moving average of lows (MAL) tends to find support.

2. *When the trend of prices is down, the MAC tends to act as resistance.* In bear trends, as price rallies to the top of the channel, the moving average of highs (MAH) tends to serve as resistance.

3. *When price bars are completely outside the top of the channel, the price trend is strongly bullish.* Please refer to Figure 8-1.

4. *When price bars are completely below the bottom of the channel, the price trend is very bearish.* See Figure 8-1.

Figures 8-2 and 8-3 further illustrate the relationship between the MAC high and low and prices. Please note that we have indicated support and resistance levels accordingly. Are you getting any ideas as to how these levels might be used?

HOW SUPPORT AND RESISTANCE DEVELOP

Please examine Figure 8-4. As the market trend continues in its existing direction, prices tend to "bounce off" their support levels, and decline from their resistance levels. The purpose of the channel is to define precise areas of support and resistance. In an uptrend, the trader will attempt to buy when price enters a support area. In a downtrend the trader will attempt to sell short when price enters a resistance area.

The key is to specifically define the following, as previously stated.

- *The trend:* An uptrend develops once there have been two or more successive price bars completely above the top of the MAC. A downtrend develops when there have been two or more successive bars below the bottom of the MAC.

- *Support and resistance:* In an uptrend, the trader will place an order to buy at the MAC low. In a downtrend, the trader will place an order to sell short at the MAC high.

- *Risk:* Risk will be a predetermined dollar amount. For less risk, use a 10 percent closing basis stop of the price at which you entered the stock. For more aggressive traders, a sell signal will get you out of your long position or a buy signal will get you out of your short position.

See Figures 8-4 through 8-10 for specific examples of this approach.
As you can see from the illustrations, traders will have many opportunities to establish positions. Regardless of whether you trade conservatively or

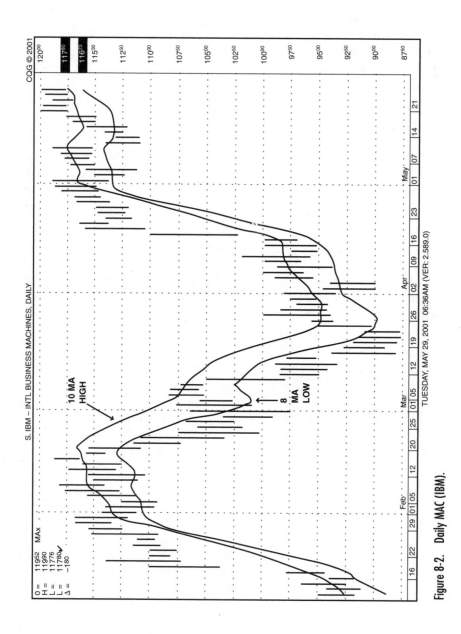

Figure 8-2. Daily MAC (IBM).

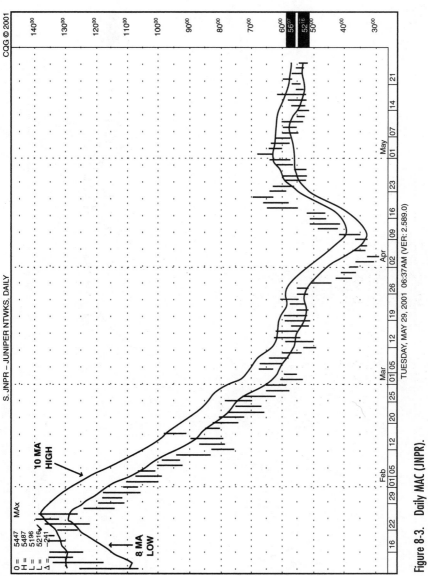

Figure 8-3. Daily MAC (JNPR).

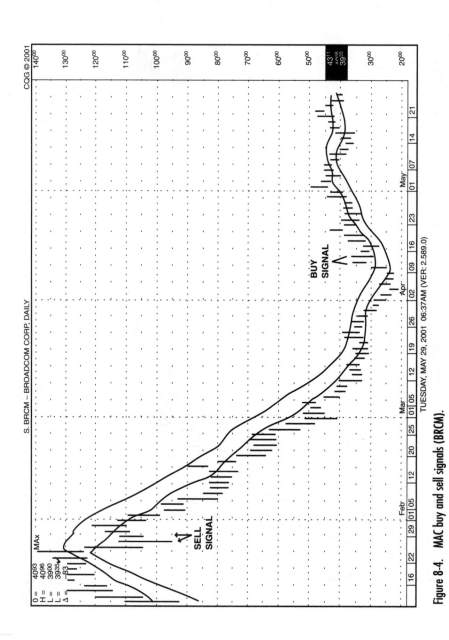

S. BRCM – BROADCOM CORP, DAILY

CQG © 2001

TUESDAY, MAY 29, 2001 06:37AM (VER: 2.589.0)

Figure 8-4.   MAC buy and sell signals (BRCM).

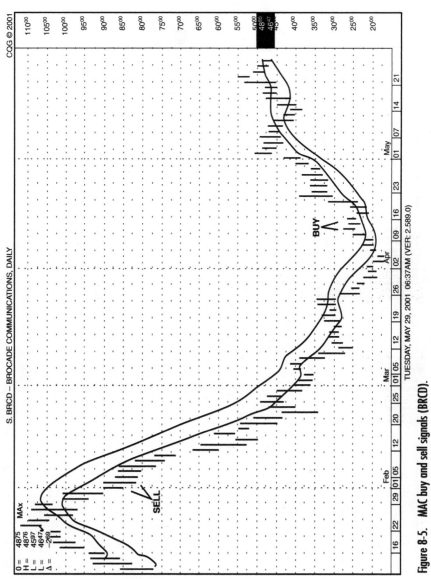

Figure 8-5. MAC buy and sell signals (BRCD).

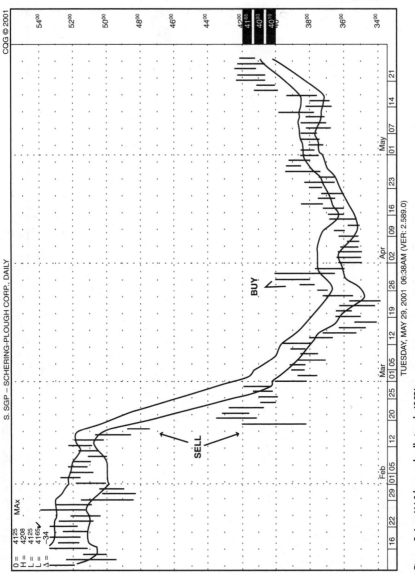

S. SGP – SCHERING-PLOUGH CORP., DAILY   CQG © 2001

O = 4125   MAx
H = 4208
L = 4125
L = 4165
Δ = -34

SELL

BUY

TUESDAY, MAY 29, 2001 06:38AM (VER: 2.589.0)

Figure 8-6.   MAC buy and sell signals (SCP).

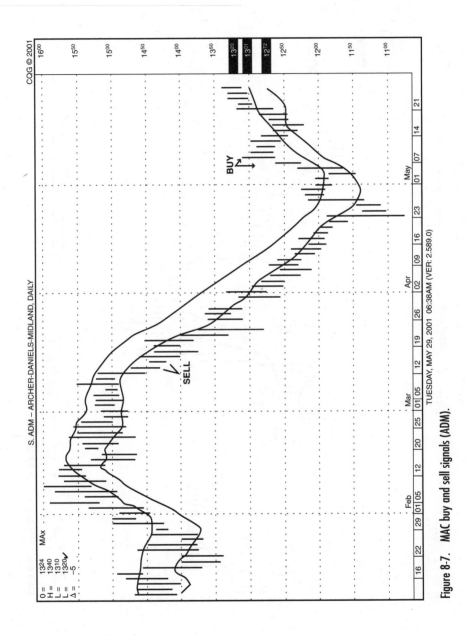

Figure 8-7. MAC buy and sell signals (ADM).

103

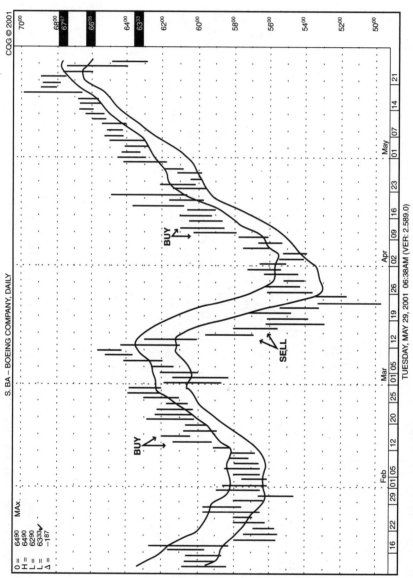

Figure 8-8. MAC buy and sell signals (BA).

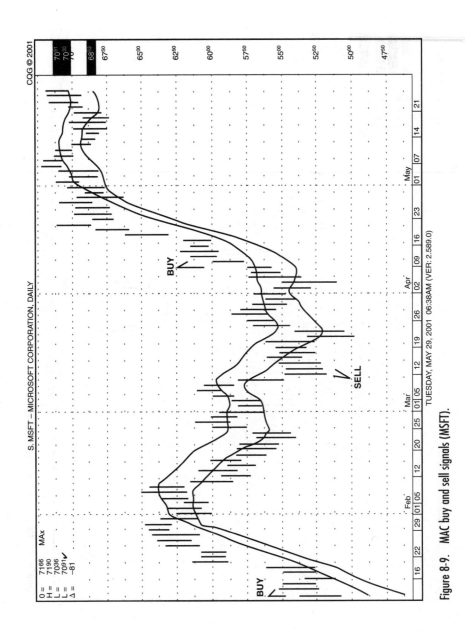

Figure 8-9. MAC buy and sell signals (MSFT).

105

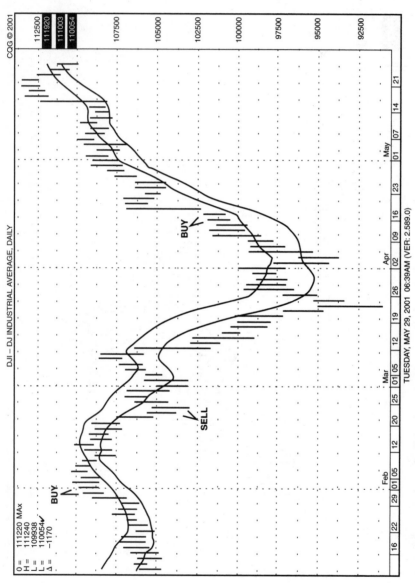

Figure 8-10.   MAC buy and sell signals (Dow Jones).

aggressively, you must trade with the trend as defined by the two-successive-bar breakout. You are only limited in the number of times you trade by your ability and your resources.

FIVE SUCCESSIVE BARS

One exceptionally interesting aspect of this approach is its ability to give you advance indication of a potentially strong rally or severe decline. In particular, five successive price bars above the top of the channel tend to forecast a very strong rally in the near future. In fact, the larger number of successive bars above the top of the channel, the stronger the move is likely to be. Numerous successive bars (five or more) below the bottom of the channel frequently forecast a large decline in the very near future.

Figures 8-11 through 8-15 illustrate this tendency. It should be noted that the earlier this pattern develops at the start of a new trend, the more likely it is to be correct. Why do we illustrate this pattern for you? Simply because this pattern will help you stay in a position longer if you know that a large move is yet to come.

EXITING POSITIONS, RIGHT OR WRONG

We've told you how and when to get in, now how do you get out? We have already suggested two stop-loss methods you can use. Here are some specifics as to the application of risk management with the MAC.

*   *Stop-loss:* The procedure here is simple enough. You have two choices. Either set a predetermined dollar risk stop-loss, which will vary from market to market, or exit on technical action.

    If you enter a long position on a decline to the MAC low, then you can exit if there are two consecutive bars outside the MAC high, which would, of course, constitute a sell signal.

    If you enter a short position on a rally to the MAC high, then you can exit if there are two consecutive bars outside the MAC high, which would, of course, constitute a buy signal.

*   *Trailing stop-loss:* Trailing stop-losses should be used once a position has started to move strongly in your favor. I have a number of suggestions to offer you in this respect, all based on extensive personal experience.

    Trail a stop-loss below the lowest low of the last three bars for long positions or above the highest high or the last three bars for short positions. This procedure has already been described. Do not use a trailing stop-loss until you show a reasonable profit. This amount varies from market to market and from trader to trader.

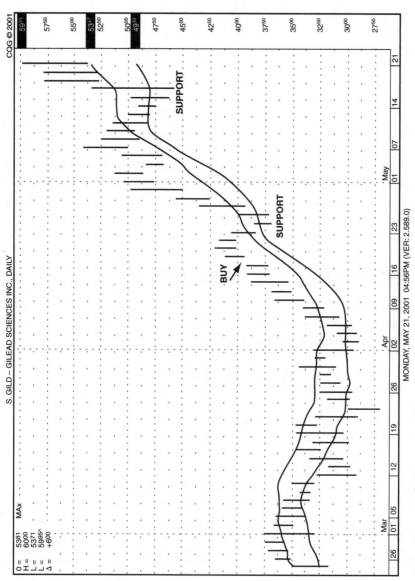

Figure 8-11. MAC five bar signals (GILD).

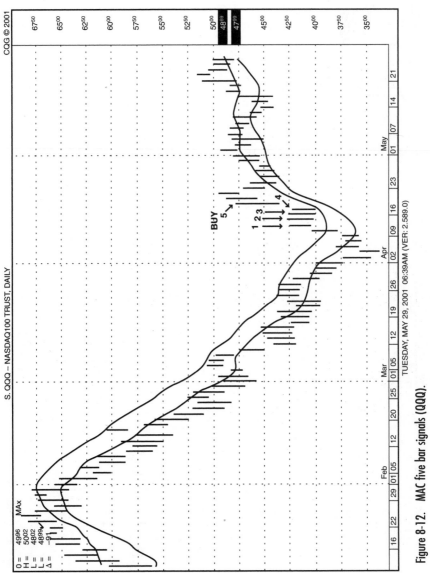

Figure 8-12. MAC five bar signals (QQQ).

109

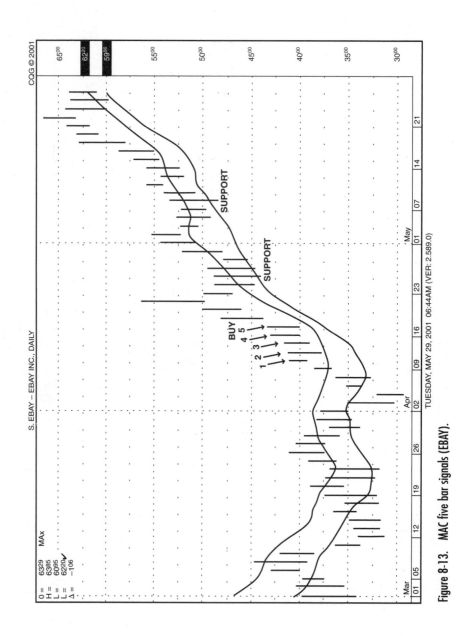

Figure 8-13. MAC five bar signals (EBAY).

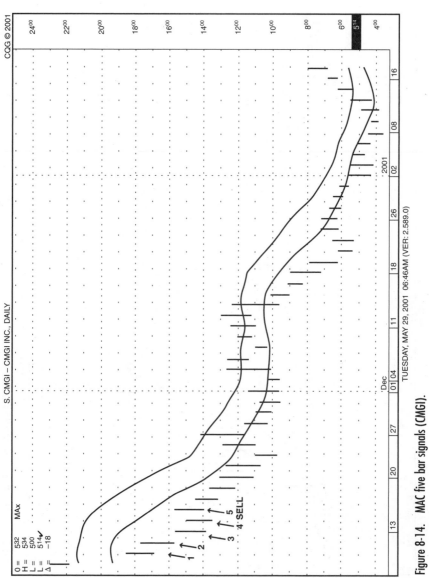

Figure 8-14.   MAC five bar signals (CMGI).

111

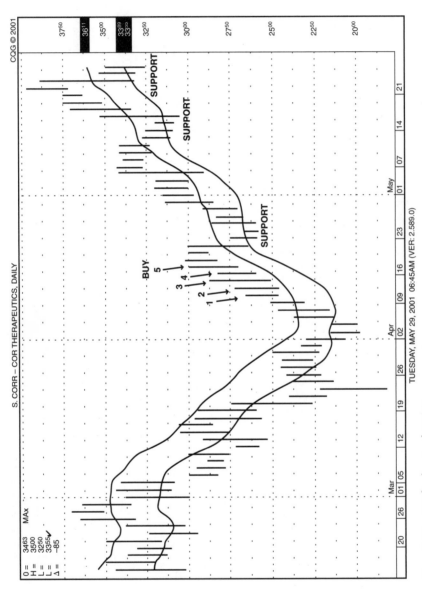

Figure 8-15. MAC five bar signals (CORR).

- *Multiple positions:* Consider multiple positions on entry so that you may have the luxury of exiting them using several different techniques. Although this may increase overall initial risk exposure, it will also allow you to capitalize on strong trends that are consistent with your position.

CHANNEL SURFING

Another good procedure for using the MAC as a short-term trading vehicle is to trade within the channel. This simply means that in an uptrend, you will attempt to buy retracements to the moving average of the lows and exit these positions when prices have rallied to the moving average of the highs or higher. Then, when prices decline once again to the moving average of the lows (if they do), you will buy again, hoping to sell on a rally to the moving average of the highs or higher.

When selling at the MAC high in a downtrend, the trader will attempt to take profits when prices decline to the MAC low, hoping to reestablish short positions on a rally to the MAC high. Both of these procedures, however, tend to limit profits, since you are cutting profits short, not knowing whether the trend will continue in your favor. This approach has been given the descriptive name *channel surfing* because you are, in effect, surfing within the channel highs and lows.

The best time to use the above technique is when there is a sideways trend. In other words, when the market is moving relatively sideways within the MAC, this technique can allow you to trade many times, buying MAC support and selling MAC resistance. As an example, Figures 8-16 through 8-20 illustrate the channel surfing method. We believe that channel surfing can be a very effective approach for the new trader who is concerned about holding a position for too long.

A FEW PRECAUTIONS AND SUGGESTIONS

Because the MAC technique we have just described is a trading method and not a system, you must be aware that it is adjustable to the needs of the trader and will not work in the same fashion for all traders who use it. Once you begin to use this technique, you will develop individual adaptation to the methodology, which may suit your purposes better than what has been described herein.

This technique may not, in fact, be suitable for all traders. You must find your own place with it, and you must determine whether this is the technique you wish to use. For those who are interested in trading frequently for

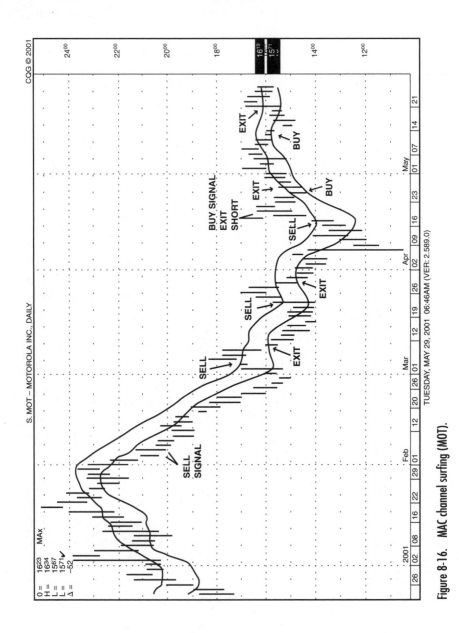

Figure 8-16. MAC channel surfing (MOT).

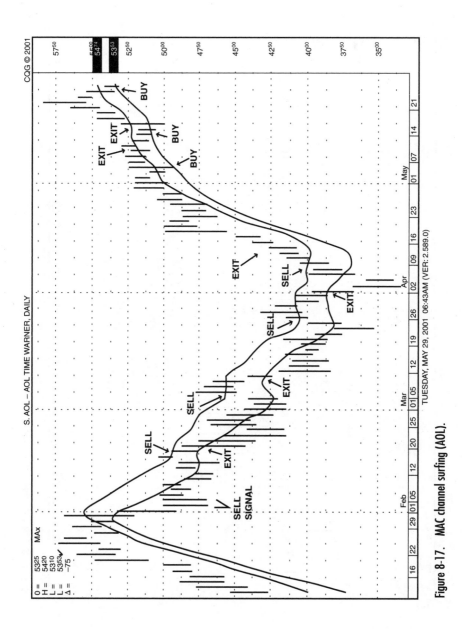

Figure 8-17. MAC channel surfing (AOL).

115

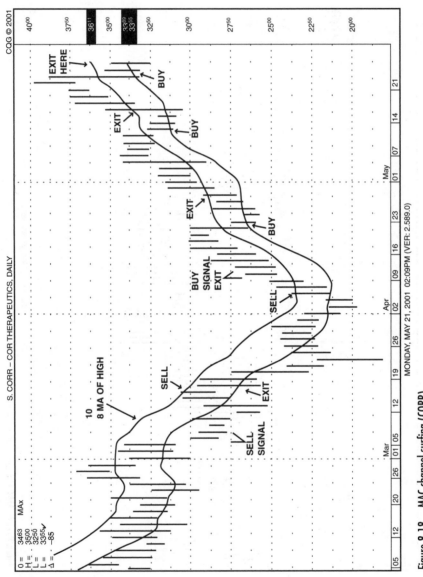

Figure 8-18. MAC channel surfing (CORR).

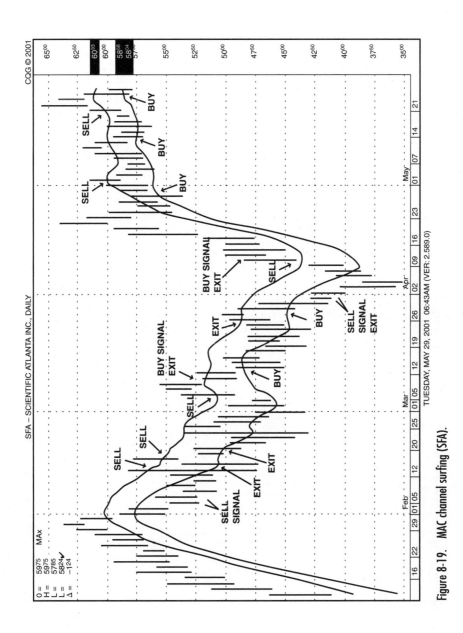

Figure 8-19. MAC channel surfing (SFA).

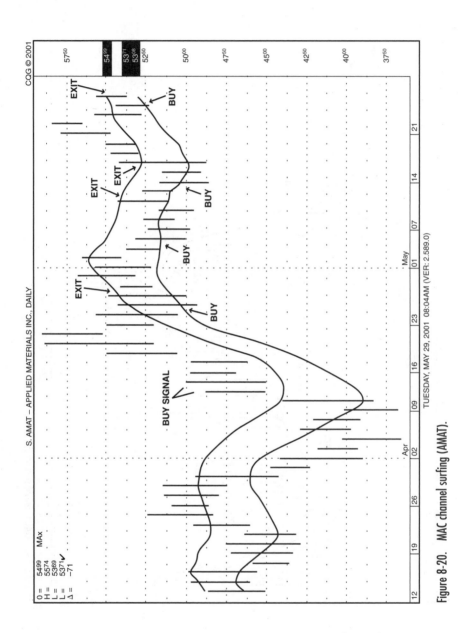

Figure 8-20. MAC channel surfing (AMAT).

small moves within a day and within an established trend, I believe that this technique is ideal. If the trend should change drastically during the day you will be stopped out of your position, and you will then, provided there is sufficient time left during the day, have the opportunity to trade from the other side of the market.

In many respects, using the MAC technique for day trading is similar to riding a bicycle. A book can only go so far in explaining to you how the job is done. Thereafter you must take the initiative, you must have the discipline, and you must take the risk in order to make the technique work for you. What I have provided in this chapter, although I have tried to be as specific as possible, is merely the framework of a technique that combines science and skill.

If you are a serious day trader who is looking for numerous opportunities to buy up support and sell at resistance, I know of few techniques that can provide as many opportunities as this one can. Yes, there will be days and there will be times when this technique does not afford you an opportunity, and there will be losing days. However, if you are consistent with it, you will find that there are many opportunities within trends to establish positions using the channel and to exit these positions profitably.

Because the channel technique is not totally mechanical and involves some degree of subjectivity, I urge you to work with it before implementing it so that you may adapt it to your particular needs and your particular style of trading.

The MAC is an excellent method for determining support, resistance, and trend. It will work well on intraday data as well as on daily, weekly, and monthly data. It does, however, require some judgment inasmuch as it is not a totally mechanical method.

SUMMARY

The moving average channel (MAC) is a method of buying stocks when they decline in an existing uptrend and selling stocks when they rally in an existing downtrend. The MAC can also tell you when a trend changes from up to down and vice versa, where support is in an uptrend, where resistance is in a downtrend, and how strong or weak a trend may be. The MAC is a very effective and specific tool that can be used in the weekly, daily, and intraday time frames for timing trend changes and for buying at support in uptrends.

CHAPTER

9

TWO REAL-TIME EXAMPLES

"Experience is a good teacher, but she sends terrific bills."

Minna Antrim

Now we will take a look at two actual trades. We'll go through all the steps I (Elliott) took in making these trades, starting from the first to the last. The examples that I am using are atypical in that they are somewhat extreme. For every one trade I make that looks like these, there are surely many that are comparatively tame.

So don't evaluate your successes and failures using these trades. But do use them as examples to learn, in a more step-by-step method, how you should be making your investment decisions. You should also remember that everybody gets lucky at times; however, if you use our decision-making techniques, we believe your chances of making profitable trades will be much higher than mere chance.

In early March 2001, I had been studying a number of alternative energy stocks. I wanted to try my hand at trading one. Previous to this trade, I had only bought one alternative energy stock called Plug Power (PLUG). I traded PLUG a number of times, but I knew that there were other alternative energy stocks that had profit potential. I intended this trade to be intermediate-term, meaning I expected to sell the stock within a month or two of my buying it. I was looking for a significant price move, at least 10 or 15 points. With this in mind, I did some research as my first step.

DOING MY HOMEWORK

Alternative energy stocks looked attractive to me for several reasons. First, I was disillusioned with many Internet and high-tech stocks. As with many investors, I had felt the burn of large declines in the Nasdaq. I thought to myself that many investors and traders would wait a while before deciding to buy such stocks again.

I had to find a sector that people would still feel comfortable trading. In addition to alternative energy, I considered biotechnology. This sector had performed well compared to the Internet sector, and its connection to the drug-manufacturing sector made people feel that although high-tech, it was somehow grounded by its relationship to a type of traditional business.

What finally pushed me toward alternative energy was the fact that California was experiencing brownouts, and that energy prices were continuing to rise. This combination of events was sure to bring energy questions into the spotlight. If a new hot sector was to emerge during the scorching summer months, alternative energy could very well be it.

I had already been studying alternative energy symbols for one of our new pages at 2chimps.com, so I had a list of about 15 symbols assembled. In order to analyze these companies, I went to CNBC.com and typed in the symbol for the alternative energy stock I was most familiar with: PLUG. From there, I got a quote, and clicked on a button that displayed several symbols similar to PLUG. I repeated this process on the symbols I found, until I had a substantial number of stocks to work with.

I tried to make sure that there was a range of active, inactive, high-priced, and low-priced stocks, so that I could capture more aspects of the alternative energy sector. I also went through each symbol and read a small company profile to make sure that each company was actually involved in alternative energy production, equipment manufacturing, and/or research and development.

At that point, I had my list of symbols completed and I had established the requirements for my trade. Now, I had to gauge which stock would work best for my purposes. As we've said before, the cheapest stocks are not always the right ones to buy. If I *had* bought a cheap stock, it's very likely that this trade would have been much less successful. I also wanted a stock with a good trading range and volume. In this case, I wanted a stock that could move at least 10 or 15 points in less than a month. I finally decided on Fuel Cell Corporation as my vehicle.

WHY FUEL CELL?

On April 10, 2001, I bought shares of Fuel Cell Corp. (FCEL) at 51.08. I decided to buy this stock for a number of reasons. I liked the fact that it was popular among traders. FCEL frequently traded over 1 million shares a day. I looked at a number of charts and saw that FCEL had the potential to trade over 2 million shares a day. I also liked the price and price movement. At 51.00 a share it had fallen significantly from its 52-week high of 108.75. FCEL still remained at a high enough price so that it could rise (or fall) as much as 10 points in a few days. In this respect, FCEL met, if not surpassed, the standards I had set for the stock I wished to trade.

This is not to say that there were no risks in trading FCEL. The company had posted no P/E ratio, which makes it hard for the investor to get a feeling for how much the stock is worth in relation to how much profit the company is making. In fact, FCEL was expected to lose 32 cents per share in the next quarter. Also, the aforementioned drop from 108.75 is not easy to stomach for some traders and investors. They may be inclined to ask, "Why shouldn't FCEL just continue on its way to the gutter?" They have a good point; there was no way to guarantee that the stock would rise once again. But I had two considerations, which both stemmed from my observations of the alternative energy sector in general. First, FCEL was losing money, but so were practically all the other companies on my list. Yes, there were symbols like GE, which have their own alternative energy ventures. These companies did have earnings. But none of the pure plays (that is, the upstart alternative energy companies I wanted to invest in) had earnings yet. There was no way I could blame FCEL for that. Second, FCEL's drop from its high was similar to the one that many of its competitors, like PLUG, experienced with the correction in the Nasdaq. Instead of disliking FCEL for its drop in price, I saw the drop as a healthy correction in an overpriced stock.

TIMING THE TRADE

The next step was to make my move. I was prepared to buy FCEL well before April 10. But I waited. In fact, I saw FCEL move from about 44.00 up to 51.08 *before* I bought. But I could not let those gains tempt me to jump in without reason. I used several timing indicators to help me decide when exactly to buy.

Looking at the chart provided (Figure 9-1), you might think, "What an idiot! He could have gained 7 points by buying a few days earlier than he did!" But that's 20:20 hindsight. If I had had the chart you're looking at, I probably would have bought earlier too! But all the information I had was what my indicators were giving me. And what they told me was, "If you buy now, FCEL may still fall." There was no way for me to be confident that my trade would be successful without my indicators giving me the buy signal. Furthermore, by using my own judgment as opposed to an objective method, the trade loses its methodology and I have no valid reason to buy or sell the stock, theoretically making it harder for me to reproduce the results in the future.

For this trade, I used two of my favorite moving average indicators, the 3-6-10 moving average and the parabolic moving average. I plotted these indicators on a customizable price chart of FCEL at the end of every trading day using bigcharts.com. As I discuss the decisions I made based on the information these indicators gave me, please refer back to Chapter 6 as needed. The three solid lines running behind the bars are the 3-, 6-, and 10-day moving averages for FCEL, while the dot trails, which appear above and below the price bars, are the parabolic moving average.

What happened on the evening of April 9 that made me decide to buy FCEL? I had not seen any reports on the news nor had I read any magazine articles or heard any gossip concerning FCEL, let alone any other alternative energy stock. Rather, I made a completely timing indicator–based decision to buy FCEL the next morning. I had watched for several days as my 3-6-10 moving average had become narrower and narrower and my parabolic had moved ever closer to the price bar. The buy signal came at the end of the trading on the 9th, when the 3- and 6-day moving average lines crossed above the 10-day moving average line. I had not yet seen my parabolic indicator switch to a buy signal (which would entail the price bar going above the plotted dot). However, from experience with these two indicators, I knew that the parabolic lagged behind the 3-6-10, and would most likely give a buy signal within a couple of days.

So I bought. The first few days that I owned FCEL, price movements and volume were not particularly impressive. There were times when I had doubts about owning the stock. I thought that if FCEL could not move soon, its upward price movements could dwindle until it began to lose value. Because I had never owned this stock before, I was not completely comfortable with my position.

But every time I had such doubts (which happened every day or two), I would look at a price chart with my indicators. Looking at the chart and seeing that my indicators still showed FCEL in an uptrend gave me the confidence to hold my shares instead of selling them. On the 27th to the 28th of April, I saw FCEL's first big price jump since I went long. It had gained slowly from 51 to 60 by the 26th, but by the end of the day on the 28th, FCEL's price was almost $70 per share.

SAFETY FIRST

I was already willing to call my FCEL trade a potentially major success, "potential" because I hadn't sold yet. It was well understood, after the "dot-com" fiasco, that even 200 percent gains could turn into losses within a matter of days. For safety's sake, I decided to use a 15 percent trailing stop-loss. In other words, at that point I was willing to give back 15 percent of my profits from the highest price FCEL had reached while I owned it. This would protect my profit.

Now you may be saying to yourself, "OK, he used his beloved indicators to tell him when to buy. If he's so infatuated with the 3-6-10 moving average, why is he using a stop-loss to tell him when to sell?" I'll let you in on a little secret. Because moving averages are lagging indicators, the 3-6-10 would tell me to sell after the stock had reversed its uptrend. And that could be a long time, causing me to give back a substantial portion of my profit. Instead of using my indicator to give me a sell signal, I decided that once I had achieved my goal for this trade (a 10- or 15-point move), I would secure my profit with the trailing stop-loss.

I continued to enter my trailing stop-loss every day beginning on the 27th of April, at which point FCEL had already made a significant gain, until the 23rd of May, making only one change. I had my eye on the Nasdaq as well. A bearish indicator in that market had made me a little more apprehensive about my more speculative positions. I tightened my stop from 15 to 10 percent. On May 23, FCEL dropped to about $81 per share, from a high of almost 95 only days before. I was stopped out of my position at 81.60. In the following days, FCEL would rebound to over $88 per share, but I couldn't complain. I was left with a total move of 30.52 points (62.5 percent), which was more than satisfactory.

ANOTHER EXAMPLE

Not every trade feels quite that good. As you will find out, some of your trades will be more of the pleasure mixed with pain variety. This is quite true for the next trade that I will examine. Falling from 51.50 to 1.0625 in less than a year, Priceline.com (PCLN) could have caused me much more pain than it did. But the hurt I felt was less the kind that destroys one's portfolio and more the kind that gives one a distinctly Pavlovian shock.

While I was having fun researching alternative energy stocks, I was also taking a little free time each day to gawk at the laughably low prices of some of the fallen "dot-com" stocks. Although I knew that these stocks retained little of the sex appeal that they had had only 6 months earlier, I still saw the potential for traders to give them a significant price boost when the Nasdaq turned around. I was watching PCLN, among other $2 to $4 Internet stocks. On April 9, only a day before I bought FCEL, I decided to buy PCLN. I had been watching PCLN for a week or longer, but I did not buy on the day that my indicator gave me the buy signal. I had no valid technical reason for my actions. The only reason I bought on April 9 instead of on March 30 was that my money was committed to other stocks.

However, when I did have the capital I needed, I took a look at my indicators and decided that I hadn't missed the move yet. Also, judging from the movement of the Nasdaq, I saw the beginning of a turnaround. This would create the right conditions for a successful rally in PCLN.

I took my position in PCLN at 2.91. I waited and watched for several weeks, checking my indicators every day or two. When the stock ended lower for the day, I would be sure to check my indicators to make certain that it hadn't given sell signals. By May 1, PCLN had risen to over $6 per share. The day after that, it had risen to nearly $8. My stock had gained about 250 percent in value. But my indicators didn't tell me to sell. I held PCLN with the intention to sell when I received the appropriate signal.

If you check a historical chart of PCLN, you can probably see why this trade was a learning experience for me. I had the chance to sell near 8 for a huge profit. Deciding to hold my shares on May 2, without a stop-loss or any other means of risk management was my biggest mistake. On May 18, I sold my shares for 4.94. Although my position made a sizable gain of about 170 percent, I had lost the opportunity to make a bigger profit.

What went wrong? I failed to use a risk management method to secure my profits. I let them slip away. After I saw such a huge profit disappear, I even forgot to check my indicators because I was disappointed about my losses and therefore lost my discipline as well.

I was lucky that I had an opportunity to sell at nearly 5 instead of selling at 4. After all, if I had sold in response to indicator signals, I would

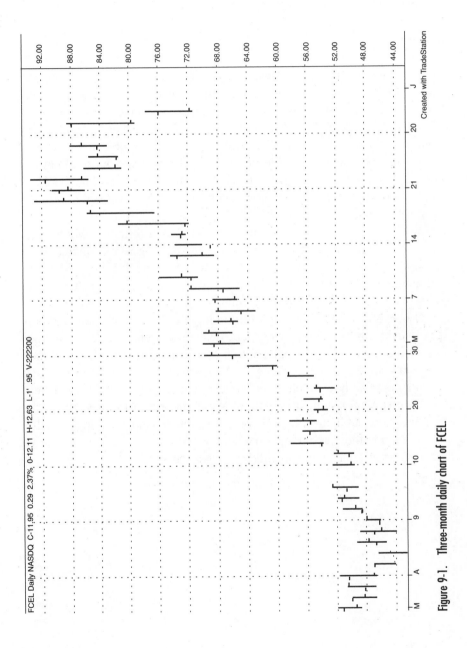

FCEL Daily NASDQ C-11.95 0.29 2.37% 0-12.11 H-12.63 L-1'.95 V-222200

Created with TradeStation

Figure 9-1. Three-month daily chart of FCEL.

have been out of my trade on May 7th or 8th, at a much better price. This trade, although profitable in the end, did not leave me feeling successful. I was determined to find every mistake that I made.

SUMMARY

The first major difference between my FCEL trade and my PCLN trade was my vision. When I decided to make my trade in FCEL, I asked myself, "What do I want out of this trade?" The answer was clear and concise. I wanted to buy a stock for a 10- to 15-point move. On the other hand, when I bought PCLN, I did significantly less thinking. My objective was less clear. I did not have a tangible price goal. My goal was more along the lines of, "I think it could double." Once it did double, I didn't know if I had reached my goal. I wasn't sure how much of my profit I wanted to protect. In short, my plan was too loose!

When I bought FCEL, the situation was much different. My actions were much more systematic. I always had a tangible goal by which I could gauge the success of my trade. Once I reached my goal, I did not have to sell automatically. However, I did know that from the point I achieved my goal forward, I had to guard my profits.

By comparing these two styles of trading, we have gained some important insights into making investment decisions. Being clear about your goals is paramount. It's acceptable to try for a small profit at first and then to see how much more you can gain. Just make sure not to be greedy and unrealistic about how much more you can gain after your goal is reached.

Using proper risk management to avoid major catastrophes takes a little more time, but in the long run you'll be a much happier camper. Finally, if you're not the risk-taking type and you prefer to sell once you've achieved your goals, you can still be very successful.

IMPLEMENTING MARKET STRATEGIES

"A good example is the best sermon."
Benjamin Franklin

USING MOM/MA

One of our favorite indicators is the 28-period momentum moving average (MOM/MA). This indicator combines a 28-period momentum with a 28-period moving average derivative of that momentum. In this section, we will discuss a number of trades that we made in real time using MOM/MA. In doing so, we hope to provide you with a realistic representation of this particular trading method and thus prepare you for using it on your own.

As you will recall, the MOM/MA method signals a buy when momentum crtosses above its MA and a sell when momentum crosses below its MA.

We begin our first example in late March 2001. During the last several trading days of the month, Chinadotcom Corp. (CHINA, Figure10-1) gave a buy signal. Momentum had risen above its moving average. Although we did not buy CHINA when it gave this signal, we still watched the stock closely. A sell signal came over a month later on May 29, when CHINA's 28-day momentum fell below the moving average plotted on our MOM/MA chart. During the span of this move, CHINA had risen from about 2.00 to 3.40. Our MOM/MA indicator told us to buy around 2.25 and to sell at 3.25, making a 1.00 or 44 percent gain.

CHINA was a big winner by the end of May. But it was time for technology stocks to take some heat. Between June and July, CHINA lost a majority of the gains made during April and May. We were done with our waiting on the sidelines. We decided to get in on the next buy signal. We bought on July 11, at 2.55. Momentum had once again crossed above its moving average, and CHINA was looking strong.

Only days later, on July 13, we took profit on our position, selling at 3.85. Our expectations for the trade had been met and far surpassed, even though MOM/MA had not given a sell signal. During the following days, we remained confident in our decision to sell, as the stock returned to where we had bought it.

Analysis

The CHINA trade discussed above was highly profitable. However, there are still those who would take issue with our decisions. As we've said before, we use technical indicators such as MOM/MA to determine when to buy and sell stocks. However, during the CHINA trade, we took some liberties in deciding how to interpret the MOM/MA signals.

If you take a close look at the chart provided (see Figure 10-2), you may notice that momentum crossed its moving average, not on July 11, but two days before on the 9th. Why did we decide to buy two days after the signal was given? Simply put, to be safe. There are strict technicians who would argue that one must buy when a signal is given, not before and not after. However, false signals do occur, and we like to weed out such signals by giving our indicator a couple of extra periods to confirm itself.

In this case, the strict technician would have bought on the 9th, between about 2.50 and 2.40. Our buy signal was not false, but the stock price did fall on the 10th. Some traders with large positions may have been stopped out of this trade, because risk had become too large as CHINA approached the low of the 10th at a price of approximately 2.30.

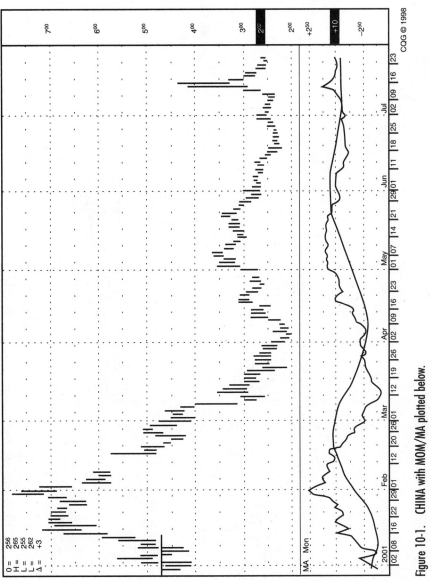

Figure 10-1. CHINA with MOM/MA plotted below.

CQG © 1998

131

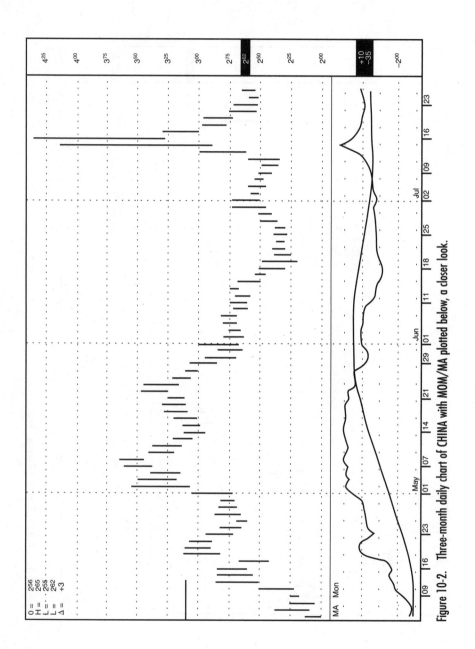

Figure 10-2. Three-month daily chart of CHINA with MOM/MA plotted below, a closer look.

132

The other major (and probably more important) criticism that strict technicians might have with our trade is our decision to sell on the 13th. There was no sell signal on our MOM/MA chart. Quite the contrary, momentum had continued to move further up and away from its moving average. In fact, most technical traders would have continued to hold CHINA for days after we sold. Such people would not criticize us for the success or failure of our trade. Rather, their quarrel would be with our technique. For many technicians, there would have been absolutely no reason to sell when we did. Their trade ends only when momentum once again falls below its moving average.

We, on the other hand, did have a motive to sell: to make money. Although it is highly important to remain objective while trading stocks, there is also a point at which personal judgments are appropriate. Let's backtrack a little, so you can understand why our decision to take a profit was logical. Before making our trade, we had a conversation about our goals for the CHINA trade. We answered several key questions, to which one should always have answers before entering a trade. You should type the following questions into a document on your computer, write your answers to the questions before entering each trade, and store them to remind yourself of your goals:

1. How many shares do we want to trade?
2. With this number of shares, how far must the stock move to cover your trading costs (i.e., commission and fees)?
3. At what point will the trade become profitable?
4. How long are you willing to hold this stock?
5. Is the price at which you will make a profit a reasonable and realistic movement considering the amount of time you are willing to hold the one stock?
6. What is your profit target and is this target reasonable and realistic considering the amount of shares you own, the past price movements of the stock, and the amount of time you are willing to hold the stock?
7. What is the maximum loss you are willing to take on this trade?

With the above questions answered, our expectations for the CHINA trade were clear. Assuming we would buy at the market price of about 2.50, we felt that a profit target of 3.00 would be reasonable. We call this price "reasonable" for several reasons. First of all, we examined CHINA's volatility for the previous year and decided that even at the low price of 2.50, the stock still had a large enough trading range to easily move $0.50.

Second, the number of shares we had decided to trade made a move of $.50 profitable. In fact, we decided that at $3.00 per share, we would be happy enough with our profits to take a profit. Finally, we agreed to hold the stock until one of three situations occurred:

1. We were satisfied with our profits.
2. We were unwilling to take more of a loss.
3. Our MOM/MA indicator gave us a sell signal.

Given these factors, the price of $3.00 per share seemed to be both a reasonable and realistic goal for our trade.

Now let's return to our trade. On the day that our profit target was met, we sold. You may have noticed that we actually got out of this trade $.85 above our target. This was due to the intraday fluctuations. Once the price of $3.00 was hit, we began to watch the market closely. We decided that because the market still looked strong, we would hold our shares until later in the day. This decision paid off and we sold at $3.85. The market continued to rise for the rest of the day and during the first few hours of the next trading day. But as the Nasdaq cooled off, so did CHINA. Over the next several days, CHINA's stock price fell back to near where we initially bought. Using a combination of a price target and a technical indicator served us well.

A good portion of the profits from our CHINA trade came from micromanagement. Instead of placing a limit order at our target price and accepting our target price as the point of maximum potential profit, we began to watch the market as soon as the price of $3.00 was hit. This allowed us to assess market conditions on a short-term basis.

Summary
By now, you should be able to understand why we feel comfortable taking profits without MOM/MA indicating a sell. Our goal is not to teach you abstract theories about price fluctuations in the stock market. Nor is it to develop trading systems that will tell you the precise moment to buy and sell for maximum profit every time. Our goal is to teach you trading methods that work. We want to help you make money. There is currently no system or strategy that will give you positive results 100 percent of the time. As you have seen, systems like MOM/MA can be slow in giving buy and sell signals and can even give false signals. This is why we advocate the use of common sense and goal setting when trading. Trying to perfect a system is an admirable undertaking, but for the investor who wishes to make money, it is not always the most profitable one.

There are those who would argue that such a combination of methods causes us to lose our objectivity. When investors begin to think about price targets and profits, they also begin to feel emotional about their money and thus make irrational decisions. We feel that trading goals do not make traders lose their objectivity. Just as technical indicators are logical and mathematical, so are trading goals. They provide a supplementary logic to trading methods, which technical indicators tend to lack. Our CHINA trade is a shining example of how setting trading goals can provide this kind of logic to your trades. Now let's change gears dramatically and look at a long-term strategy.

DOLLAR COST AVERAGING WITH MUTUAL FUND INVESTMENTS

There are a number of ways you can go about investing in mutual funds. Which method you choose can be crucially important to the success or failure of your long-term investments. Because of the long-term nature of mutual fund investments, careful consideration should be given to how you decide when to buy, when to dollar cost average (DCA) into the mutual funds you choose, and when to sell. This section will provide a comparison between a popular method of mutual fund investment using DCA and our mutual fund investment strategy using DCA with technical indicators.

The examples we use in this section are not based on investments we actually made. We feel that they are, however, accurate representations of mutual fund investment strategies that you can use. Each strategy has its own pros and cons. You can experiment on your own, if you like, with historical data or actual investments. But no matter what you decide, after all is said and done, make sure you continue to DCA into your long-term investment.

The fund we have decided to use in this example is the Rydex Biotechnology Fund (RYOIX). This fund has been trading since May 1998. It has been particularly volatile compared to the vast majority of mutual funds. Therefore, we do not see it as a suitable investment vehicle for everyone. We use RYOIX in our examples because its volatility allows us to illustrate how you may be able to see the differences between the two investment methods presented. With long-term investments, which may last decades, such differences may be greatly amplified. Now, let's begin our comparison.

Investing in RYOIX Biquarterly
This method of investment may appear rather basic, and it is. We begin investing on August 13, 1998, only a few months after the inception of

RYOIX. Our strategy is to invest $250 every other quarter, so that we make two investments in RYOIX per year, regardless of price. On August 13, 1998 we purchase 28.31 shares at $8.83 per share.

The second investment is made on February 12, 1999, two quarters later. On that date, we purchase 21.21 shares at $11.79 for another $250. This investment process continues. Every half-year we invest $250, whether the price seems high or low.

Our biquarterly investment data table (Table 10-1) shows the exact dates, prices, and number of shares that we would have purchased. With the biquarterly investment strategy, we invested six times, buying a total of 76.257 shares at an average cost of $18.67 per share.

Investing in RYOIX with Indicators

The second method is a little more complicated. This method combines the traditional DCA method with any number of technical indicators. While we use MOM/MA in this specific example, you are free to use any of your favorite indicators in your mutual fund investment decisions. Because of the long-term nature of these investments, leading, time concurrent, and lagging indicators should all work. Just beware of false signals if you choose to use "fast" indicators. Making mistakes in your long-term invest-ment strategy can cost you dearly over time.

In our example, we begin watching RYOIX 42 days after it begins trading. Because we are investing over a long period of time, we prefer a slower indicator with fewer false signals. Therefore, we use our normal MOM/MA indicator, with a 42-period momentum and MA, rather than the usual 28-period momentum and MA. We also make one extra rule. In order to further weed out false signals, we consider a buy signal valid only if it remains bullish for ten periods in a row. The data table for the second

TABLE 10-1. BIQUARTERLY INVESTMENT DATA TABLE		
Date	**Price**	**No. of Shares**
8/13/98	$ 8.83	21.204
2/12/99	11.79	15.024
8/13/99	16.64	15.024
2/14/00	31.73	7.879
8/14/00	31.92	7.832
2/13/01	26.90	9.294
Total shares		76.257

method (Table 10-2) has two date columns: the first with the initial signal date and the second with the buy date, ten trading days later.

With our system clearly defined, we get ready to make our first buy. On September 21, 1998, we spot a buy signal. Momentum has risen above its moving average. This signal remains bullish, confirming itself ten trading days later. On October 5, we make our first investment of $250 at $8.87, buying 28.18 shares. You can see the first signal on the MOM/MA chart at the bottom of Figure 10-3. We hold our shares as momentum falls below its moving average. We repeat this process when a new buy signal is given on June 14, 1999. The signal is confirmed fourteen trading days later on June 28, and we invest another $250 at the price of $12.53.

By the end of July 20, 2001, we have invested a total of $1500 in RYOIX in six increments of $250. We own a total of 92.33 shares at an average cost of $16.246.

A COMPARISON OF STRATEGIES

In making this comparison, we attempted to keep constant as many variables as possible. In each example we invest a total of $1500 over the same time period in six increments of $250. Thus, each system has an equal opportunity to determine average cost and total number of shares purchased. But merely discussing these strategies in terms of dates and prices does not do them justice. We must also examine the requirements each system has on the trader.

As we said before, the biquarterly investment is simple. It is a mechanical method that does not require the investor to look at price charts, eval-

TABLE 10-2. DATA TABLE FOR METHOD COMBINING DCA WITH OTHER TECHNICAL INDICATORS

Signal Date	Buy Date	Price	No. of Shares
9/21/98	10/05/98	$ 8.87	28.184
6/14/99	6/28/99	12.53	19.952
11/17/99	12/02/99	17.24	14.501
5/16/00	5/31/00	23.88	9.356
1/18/00	1/31/01	28.17	9.232
4/12/01	4/27/01	23.98	11.106
Total shares			92.331

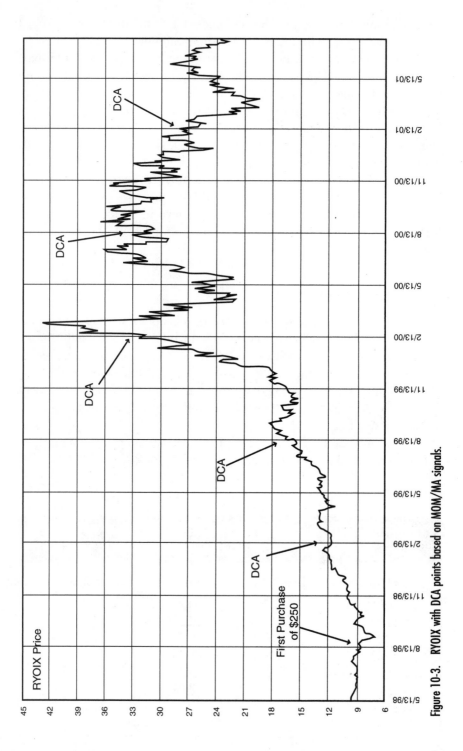

Figure 10-3. RYOIX with DCA points based on MOM/MA signals.

uate timing indicators, or make any other judgments. All he or she must do is have the money ready to invest and know on which day to invest it.

This method presents a number of advantages to the undisciplined investor. If you feel nervous about making decisions about when to invest or why, this method decides for you! No calculations, no waiting, no price watching. Furthermore, with this method, you will be investing on a regular basis. As long as you consistently have the money to invest, no period longer than half a year will go by without your making some type of investment.

However, when you decide to use this method, you are also resigning yourself to the notion that you cannot beat the market. But the fact of the matter is that there *are* better times and worse times to buy, and you *can* do something about it. All it takes is patience and discipline.

Using a combination of timing indicators and DCA is the proactive investor's strategy for long-term investing in mutual funds and stocks. It leaves you in control to buy when you wish, and potentially to have a better average price for your investments.

Without a doubt, this method has its risks. The MOM/MA indicator can give false signals (as can any timing indicator). Between the period of September 10, 2000, and April 10, 2001, approximately thirteen false buy signals were given. Even though our two-period confirmation rule weeded out most of these signals, we still bought on December 18, 2000, one day after which our indicator gave a sell. Whether this is in fact a false signal or not is questionable. After all, there were ten periods in which our signal remained bullish. There is no special method of solving such problems. But put into perspective, the problem is not horribly big. Our five good fills and one mediocre fill still left us with a low DCA. And in the end, that's what matters.

Most other risks associated with this method are linked to investor behavior. You can effectively neutralize such risks by remaining disciplined. There will be times when your technical indicators do not allow you to DCA into your mutual funds. Unlike the biquarterly investment method, there may be long periods, spanning from several months to a year and longer, when you will not invest more money in your funds. And, vice versa, there may be instances where your indicators tell you to buy several times in a period of a couple of months. (You may want to consider slowing down your indicator if this happens several times in a row.) Because a buy signal could appear at any time, you must have your money ready to invest. If you choose to invest in chunks of $250, as we did in our example, you must always have another $250 ready to invest. Once you buy into your fund, be sure to have your next sum of $250 in your account within a few days.

WRAP UP

Nobody wants a mediocre average cost for long-term investments. Such costs become more and more of a burden as you continue to DCA into your investments. Biquarterly investment is easy, simple, and requires the least amount of discipline. But even in the market, the less you give, the less you will receive. Try putting in a little more effort and even in a few short years, you will see the difference. Choose your favorite indicators, take a long-term perspective, and begin to DCA into mutual funds. You won't need to look at your funds every day. You might want to look at them once a week. If you follow our strategy for using DCA with technical indicators, you could be reaping the rewards for years to come.

SUMMARY

This chapter examined a number of trading strategies in depth. We showed you how each strategy works in terms of real trading and investing. Each example was intended to facilitate a discussion about the real benefits and drawbacks of the strategies we provide for you in this book.

11

THE IMPORTANCE OF DISCIPLINE: MAXIMIZING PROFITS, MINIMIZING LOSSES, FOLLOWING THE RULES

"When things are steep remember to stay level-headed."
Horace

No matter what tasks you set for yourself, the key to realizing your goals is just as much the result of perseverance and self-discipline as it is of technique and methodology. In other words, you can use a very effective trading method but if it is not applied or implemented in a consistent and thorough fashion, then it will not work for you. On the other hand, you can use a very average system or method, one that shows only mediocre results in historical testing, but it can perform well for you if it is implemented with discipline and consistency.

Whether you seek to excel as a writer, a trader, a doctor, or an investor, you will rarely achieve your goals through luck. You will most often arrive at your goal destination through the application of time-tested rules that are applied consistently, repeatedly, diligently, and with discipline. Too many investors and traders believe that success is merely a matter of learning strategies that work. While the name of this book is *Stock Market Strategies that Work*, the title is somewhat incomplete. The subtitle should read "If you use them correctly." And, this is where the all-important topic of discipline comes into play. This chapter will examine the role(s) of trading discipline—its definition, intricacies, and application.

We will begin with the premise that most investors do not understand the meaning of discipline and that discipline is a topic that unfortunately bores most investors. Hopefully, the discussion that follows will be anything but boring. Remember that this is, in many ways, the single most important chapter in this book. Unless you master your self-discipline, you will have difficulty following the suggestions in this book and the odds are that you will lose money.

TRADING DISCIPLINE: A WORKING DEFINITION

One of the main reasons so many traders find it difficult to master discipline is that they have failed to define it. In order to know your enemy you must visualize it or you'll be stabbing at ghosts. For many traders, discipline is very difficult to define. It is illusory. And without a true definition of discipline, investors will not succeed in the market. Let's begin with a working definition of t*rading discipline*.

- *Trading discipline:* Putting into action the actions generated by a trading system, method, or procedure and implementing the risk management rules that accompany that system, method, or procedure.

In simple terms, *discipline* is the ability to follow a plan. But things are not as simple as they may first appear. It's simple (perhaps too simple) to say, "Starting today I'm going to follow my investing plan and never will I vary from it." If following a plan was that simple, we would all be excellent investors and traders, and there would be no need for this chapter. If self-discipline was easy to develop or implement, then no one in this world would need dieting; diet books; solutions to alcohol, drug, or tobacco addictions; and a host of other manifestations that arise from lack of self-discipline (as one of the root causes).

Clearly, discipline is a matter of individuality. What requires great self-control and the highest level of attention by one individual is a simple matter requiring little effort by another individual. We all have our own weak points, our own Achilles heels, and our own limitations. In some individuals and in some situations, these shortcomings are very specific and easily identified whereas in other individuals they are subtle, illusory, and not readily discernible.

Because personality, background, perception, emotional predisposition, socioeconomic status, and needs vary from one individual to another, that which requires discipline and self-control for one investor in one situation may be significantly different from the effort and skill required of another investor in the same situation. Tasks that some people achieve only with considerable effort are completed in a virtually automatic fashion by others. By following the guidelines presented in this chapter, we believe that issues of discipline in investing can be overcome.

Remember that discipline is the weakest link in the chain of investment and trading success. Without discipline, success can be achieved only by luck. If luck is what you are depending on for your financial future then you will be sadly disappointed. In all your investments we urge you to remember the following three warnings. You might want to put them on a large poster or an index card and keep them handy. Ask yourself daily if you are guilty of the following "investment sins."

Any investment program or trading system will be rendered either useless, ineffective, or a losing proposition if you:

1. Lack the discipline to keep your investment research or methods up to date
2. Lack the discipline to implement your investment decisions
3. Lack the discipline to follow sound risk management

As you can see, trading discipline is multifaceted and interdependent. There are layers and levels of discipline, all of which interact to produce positive or negative results.

Let's take a closer look at the various levels of investment discipline. Before doing so, we want to add that developing investment discipline will also have beneficial effects on other aspects of your life. It will help you improve what you're doing in business and perhaps even in your personal relationships. There is nothing that can help you as much as developing a plan and sticking with it!

THE THREE LEVELS OF INVESTING DISCIPLINE

The three levels of investing discipline are as follows: preparation and planning, implementation, and risk management. As stated earlier, they are interdependent. Without one the others are either unlikely to develop or they are apt to be weak and ineffective.

Preparation and Planning

If you intend to follow a system, method, or indicator such as those taught in this book or discussed in the many books that are currently available to investors, the system must be maintained in working order. You must do your homework by keeping your work up to date and accurate if it is to serve you well with valid trading signals.

No matter what your approach may be, this level of self-discipline holds true. Whether you invest or trade on the news, on earnings reports, on an evaluation of corporate management, price charts, technical indicators, a computerized system, or all of the above, you can't be successful if your work isn't up to date.

Implementation

This is the single most difficult aspect of discipline for the vast majority of investors. While they have no trouble updating their systems, they have great difficulty implementing them. This problem is so pervasive that many books could be written on this topic alone. Failure to implement investment decisions is the result of either poor follow-through, lack of self-confidence, or fear.

Lack of follow-through can be easily remedied by trading with a partner or by implementing some of the suggestions given earlier. Lack of self-confidence and/or fear is not as easily overcome. Because each individual has his or her own personal experience(s) with what creates the fear, this must be dealt with on an individual basis.

Risk Management

This is by far the most mismanaged area of investing. Undisciplined investors and traders are grist for the mill. They are the ones who regularly contribute money to the coffers of those who are successful. Lack of effective risk management is responsible for turning small losses into large losses or for turning potentially large profits into small profits as they are "picked off the vine" prematurely.

Most investors and traders that we have observed and spoken with readily admit that their largest losing trades have most often been trades which could have been closed out as small losers, according to their trading system, but which were left too long. And they admit that they have, more often than not, exited profitable investments and trades much too soon, often leaving major money "on the table" because they failed to follow their risk management methods.

The ability to close out losers promptly and to ride winners is by far the most important of all forms of trading discipline. More investors have lost more money by riding losers than by picking bad investments that were closed out as small losses.

CLOSING OUT LOSERS

The big question is how to close out those losers. Again, the answer is simple. If you cannot close those losers out when your investment or trading method says to do so, get someone to do it for you! Along these lines, we have several suggestions:

- If your system uses a stop-loss immediately when you get into a position, then enter your stop-loss immediately as well. If the stop-loss stays the same for the duration of the investment or trade, then enter an open order (good-until-canceled).
- If your system uses a trailing stop-loss, make certain you enter the trailing stop-loss each time it needs to be changed.
- To stay honest with your system and yourself, have another investor or trader monitor your system(s) and evaluate your discipline accordingly.
- Use a checklist. Check off each item on your list as it is completed.

How to Determine What's Right for You
Goals and needs go hand in hand. In order to determine exactly how your trading discipline can be improved, there are additional questions that must be asked as part of your effort to become a profitable investor. They are as follows.

Do You Need to Improve Your Discipline?   A simple way to get the correct answer to this question is to look at your investing results. By answering the questions below you'll get a quick idea of whether your trading discipline needs improvement.

- Are your results in real time different from the ideal performance of your system or method?
- Are you making money?
- Are you losing money when your system says you should be making money?
- Did the stock market go in the direction that you expected?
- Have you made money from your expectations?

If you are not performing as your system would ideally have you do, and if you are not profiting from your signal and/or projections, it is likely that your discipline is at fault. If, however, you are satisfied with your profits, and if you are trading in accordance with your plans and system, no changes in discipline are warranted at this time.

Can You Isolate the Source(s) of Your Losses?

- *Determine the reason(s) for your losses.* This means that each loss must be examined in detail.
- *Determine the cause of each loss.* Causes can fall into many different categories. They can be due to emotion, errors, disorganization, lack of sufficient margin, and a host of other variables. You will not be able to change the cause until you have determined the cause.

Can You Be Specific?

- When you investigate the cause of each loss, do so in considerable detail.
- Retrace all your steps, from the original technical signal to the actual liquidation of the trade.
- Be as specific as possible, tracking down the reason(s) for each losing trade.

Have You Kept a Diary?   Keep a diary of your investing to help delineate the quality of your discipline or lack thereof. By retracing your steps you may find the clue to your difficulty. Record the following:

1. Date, time, and price the trade was entered
2. The number of shares bought or sold
3. Reason(s) for entry (be specific)
4. Date, time, and price that trade was closed out
5. Reason(s) for exit (be specific)
6. Any thoughts, feelings, special situations, problems, or events that transpired directly before or after you entered or exited the trade

Frequently, the mere act of keeping a diary will alert you to potential or actual problems with discipline. Here are two more salient points regarding keeping a diary.

- *The best time to write in your diary is when you enter or exit a given trade.* If you are too busy, however, then update your diary at the end of the trading day.
- *We maintain that a diary is extremely important when tracking discipline.* Every trader should keep a diary, whether you are making money or losing money. A diary can be the source of much important information.

Have You Ruled Anything Out?   When you are looking for answers, consider everything. Do not rule anything out. Something as simple as talking to the wrong people can be the source of your lack of discipline.

Have You Looked for Patterns?
- Study your behavior in detail and watch for patterns and repertoire.
- Determine what event(s) came immediately before and immediately after your lack of discipline.

A CLOSER LOOK AT FEAR

As we stated earlier in this chapter, there are several types of fear. If we understand them better, we can be more successful at overcoming them. Do you have a fear of investing? Do any of the following fears sound familiar to you?

- *Fear of losses.* Fear of losses is a conscious fear. Investors will not take action when they are afraid of losing money. It's that simple. And the fear escalates with each loss until it reaches the point of complete withdrawal or inactivity. This is a normal reaction to losses. If you touch a hot stove and you get burned, you will be disinclined to touch it again.

    But, if the stove is hot sometimes and not hot at other times, you will never know when to touch it. If opening the oven door allows you to put your hand in and take money out, the dilemma is even more anxiety-provoking. It presents the classic "approach-avoidance" situation. And that's one of the most difficult problems to overcome.

    Laboratory animals in this situation are locked into inconsistent and neurotic behaviors for many years. The fact that you do not know when or if you'll make or lose money in the stock market makes this problem a severe and difficult one to overcome. But, as we have told you, there are ways!

- *Fear of profit.* There are many investors who tend to be very uncomfortable when they have been successful. These individuals fear their own impulses. In most cases their self-esteem is so diminished that they refuse to accept the reality of being a winner. Why do they continue to play the game? They do so because they have not yet come to grips with their unconscious desire to avoid winning.

  These investors are essentially normal individuals, yet they know deep down that they have never had a complete victory in their lives—that they have never thoroughly enjoyed anything. In such cases, lack of discipline is deeply rooted and must be treated by a mental health professional although it can be remedied in other ways.

Problem-Solving Suggestions

No discussion of self-discipline would be complete without suggestions as to how you might go about solving the problems that lack of discipline can create. Here are a few of our suggestions learned from long and often costly experience:

- *Have someone else do your market homework for you if you are incapable of it.* There are many individuals who enjoy following procedures and plans. Hire one of them to do the work for you if you cannot or prefer not to do it on your own with consistency.
- *Get an investing partner who will do the homework for you or get a few partners.* Investment clubs are also good for this purpose.
- *Get your trading advice from an advisory service or a trading adviser.* As simple as this "cure" may be, there are hundreds of thousands of investors who cannot follow the advice of their market expert. It becomes especially difficult for some investors to follow the advice of a newsletter or trading adviser when they are losing money. That is a real test for many.

  By having someone else do the actual investing for you, according to the recommendations of your adviser, you will avoid failing at this level. But remember that you need to find a good adviser first. And that will take time and considerable effort (and discipline).
- *Be on the lookout for unconscious errors when you do your market homework, particularly when you are on a losing streak.* You can easily make mistakes that you are not even aware of but which are the result of a negative attitude.
- *It helps to be organized.* Organization cuts down on errors. If you can't get organized, then have someone do it for you even if you have to pay for this service!

OVERCOMING THE FEAR OF INVESTING

• *Have someone else "pull the trigger" for you.* The preferred choice is a detached person who does not have a vested interest in your trading. You can recruit the help of a friend, a partner, a spouse, or even a broker. But be sure you trust them and make sure they won't be influenced by your inconsistencies.

  It might be a good idea to have a written contract with them (not necessarily as a legal document but rather as one that will set forth the rules of what you are doing and trying to accomplish).

• *Develop a system of checks and balances.* Cross-check your system with another investor who invests in a fashion that is similar to your methodology. By monitoring the same investing and signals, you can keep each other honest.

• *Take baby steps.* One of the best ways to overcome fear of investing is by taking small steps first. Don't plunge into the market with a major dollar commitment! To do so would scare you and would thereby increase your odds of making mistakes due to fear. Take things slowly.

  Invest a few hundred dollars at first. Build up your confidence. As you are more successful, take bigger steps. And reward yourself for a job well done. When you're right, allow yourself the opportunity to brag about it. Take some of your profits and spend them. The game is all about making money for the purpose of spending money (either sooner or later).

  If this approach doesn't work for you, then you may have a more serious problem and you might want to consult a mental health professional. Fear is reasonable but persistent fear and/or panic may be a clinical problem that should be treated by a professional since it can get worse and may, at times, be symptomatic of other problems in your life and/or relationships.

A FEW CLOSING THOUGHTS ABOUT DISCIPLINE

So what is the "bottom line" of the trading discipline issue? There are several points that deserve mentioning.

• *Trading discipline can be learned.* Discipline of any kind is *not* innate. We learn it as a function of exposure to various learning experiences, most of which come from our parents and teachers. While it is true that some people appear to be more organized than others are, we emphasize that *organization and discipline are not one and the same.* There are many highly organized traders who have not mastered the finer points of discipline.

- *Trading discipline is by far the weakest link in the trading chain.* Without discipline, virtually nothing is possible. Any trader who feels that he or she can achieve lasting success without trading discipline is living a lie. Any trader who fails to develop the necessary skills that are part and parcel of trading discipline is doomed to failure.

  Any trader who refuses to accept the importance of discipline in the three areas we've outlined previously is destined to fail repeatedly. Any trader who has not overcome the problems that arise as a function of poor discipline will never be successful other than through luck.

- *Trading discipline is at least as important as your trading system.* You must find ways to make the two work together for you. A system without discipline is like a ship without a rudder—it cannot be guided safely through treacherous waters. It will be dashed upon the rocks in stormy seas.

- *Trading discipline should be your priority.* Place it number one on your list, even ahead of having an effective trading system. Learn discipline first by applying some of the suggestions we have given you. Talk to successful traders and/or investors. Observe the habits of successful traders. Study your losing trades to find out where you went wrong each time you take a loss and, above all, always distinguish between losses you took as a function of poor discipline and losses you took in following a system.

  Losses from following a system are acceptable, and you will learn from them. Losses owing to poor discipline are unacceptable, and you will not grow unless you understand what it is you did that caused you to lose your discipline.

CONCLUSION

Discipline in trading is as simple as following your own trading rules and as complicated as undertaking the planning and preparation required, dealing with the fear of taking losses as well as profits, keeping careful records, and placing discipline as your top priority. Losses can only be minimized through discipline, and profits can only be maximized through discipline.

As multifaceted and interdependent as the issue of discipline in trading is, it can ultimately be learned if commitment is strong enough. The rewards for discipline are the steady day-by-day increases in profits from winning trades and the inevitable reduction in drawdown and risk.

Hopefully the foregoing discussion of discipline and its various aspects was sufficiently clear to help you overcome difficulties you may have had in this area. If you are a new investor or trader, then our guidelines will help you prepare for the challenges that await you.

SUMMARY

This chapter examined the role of discipline as an integral aspect of investing success. The various aspects of discipline were defined, and solutions were offered to several discipline problems that investors often experience. Investor discipline (or the lack thereof) is often the weakest link in the chain of investment success.

COMPUTERIZED
TRADING SYSTEMS

"640K ought to be enough for anybody."
Bill Gates in 1981

Roger is a newcomer to stock trading. Like many beginning investors, he reasons that there is nothing to gain by reinventing the wheel. There must be someone out there who has mastered the secrets of stock trading and who is willing, for a price, to share winning techniques with him. Rather than take the time to learn how to invest and trade, Roger goes to the Internet to search for stock market trading systems and computer programs that he can use to attain his goals. To his amazement, a keyword search on the term *stock market trading systems* returns 2,726,975 possibilities. He is overwhelmed but encouraged. After all, with so many possible choices he's certain to find something that works.

After several hours of searching, Roger narrows his choices down to a few programs that seem to have a number of similar features. They all claim to be highly accurate; they all claim to be very specific; they all show glowing historical results, and they all sell for over $2500. But price is no barrier for Roger. He knows that the cost of education in any field is dear. He spends a few more hours studying the various programs and then follows up his research by calling the toll-free number for each of the vendors in order to ask more questions. He realizes that his choice will not be an easy one since all of the programs appear to be very successful. He decides to wait a few days before spending his money.

BUY INTO THE MYTH

Later in the week Roger makes his purchase. Naturally he must have the system as soon as possible so he pays the additional $14 for next-day delivery. Now the fun begins! After installing his new software, he dedicates himself to the tutorial and manual. He learns how to make charts and graphs that show buy and sell signals. He learns how to run the daily report, showing which stocks the computer program wants to buy or sell. He quickly becomes familiar with the nuances of the program and is soon ready to trade.

Sadly, things do not continue well for our hero. His first five real-time trades are closed out at a loss. In spite of the supposedly high probability claimed by the program, Roger is off to a dubious start. At first he wonders if he is doing something wrong. It must be him. It can't possibly be the program! The next five trades suggest otherwise. Of the ten trades he has made, seven lost money, two were closed out at about breakeven, and one made $330. Roger is discouraged but not ready to quit. He calls the software vendor to ask some probing questions. He is advised to give the program time and money. After all, a program that bases its historical results on thousands of historical hypothetical trades cannot be judged to be successful or unsuccessful in real time after making a mere ten trades. But Roger is concerned. He fears that he may run out of money before the program begins to work. Clearly this is something he didn't anticipate. Experience is the best teacher. And it is teaching Roger what so many other investors learn the hard way. Most computerized trading programs available to investors and traders have some inherent limitations as well as some intrinsic flaws. Unless the right questions are asked (and answered) before money is risked in the market, the probability of success is fairly low.

DEFINING THE REALITY

If you have looked through any of the popular investing or trading publications, you may have seen advertisements for computerized trading systems. We're not talking about systems that simply plot charts and timing indicators for you. We're talking about programs like the one that Roger bought and attempted to use. We're talking about software programs that actually analyze stocks for you and tell you what to buy or sell and when to do it. Some of these systems make strong claims in their advertising. If you've taken the time to read the claims, you've found most of them to be quite dramatic. And the magnitude of the claims is often exceeded only by the cost of the software. One of the most popular programs sells for nearly $4000! If you've been tempted by these advertisements, in print or on the Internet, then you may want to step back for a few minutes and ask some important questions. You will need to ask questions that Roger failed to ask. But we can't fault Roger for his ignorance. Many investors are ignorant, and they pay for their ignorance with losses.

This chapter will help you know what kinds of questions to ask and what kinds of answers to look for before you spend any money on these systems. In short, you must do everything you can to verify the claims of system vendors. If you believe for even one second that all of the promises and performance statistics are true, then you are easy prey for the promoters. And while some of the claims appear to be valid on the surface, the truth is that they are the result of creative statistics. Computers can do many wonderful things, but they also allow dishonest promoters to trick uninformed investors.

LET THE BUYER BEWARE!

You may be thinking that existing government rules and regulations about advertising will protect you. After all, the Securities and Exchange Commission and other regulatory agencies must have standards and laws in place, which regulate system vendors. Yes, there are regulations, but there are also ways in which creative promoters can circumvent the rules with clever ad copy, small print, and disclaimers. Investors want to believe that there are systems out there in the market jungle that can make them rich. The popular, but not necessarily correct, belief is that if a computer is somehow involved then the results must necessarily be positive. Whatever happened to the "Garbage in— garbage out" warning? As in all things, the buyer must beware. Unless you ask the right questions, you won't get the right answers. It's that simple, and it's that complicated.

The trading public need not be victimized by the fallacious or exaggerated assertions about trading systems. While the software to test systems is readily available, it is necessary to know the essential ingredients, which comprise a successful test. Many traders today underestimate the ability of some promoters to creatively portray the performance statistics of a system. Systems developers can massage statistics in order to show favorable results. Skillful manipulation of system statistics can emphasize or even enhance the positive aspects of a system while minimizing the negatives.

But we are quick to add here that system promoters are not the only ones who can doctor their results and their systems to show optimum performance. Individual investors are also guilty at times. We all tend to deceive ourselves when testing and/or developing our own systems. High expectations, wishful thinking, and various subtle oversights can lead us all into the abyss of self-deception. All too often we tend to confuse past performance with future results. We tend to believe that a trading system that we have developed and back-tested on historical data must perform the same way in the future. And that's where we go wrong!

In order to determine the validity of any system, it is crucial to remember that simply reporting highly favorable results does not guarantee success with that system in real-time trading. The basic assumption, "The better it worked in the past, the better it will work in the future," has been one of the more costly misconceptions. Unfortunately, a common but misguided objective of many testing systems is to develop trading strategies that extract the greatest possible profit from historical data without regard for such factors as the number of consecutive losing trades, drawdown (to be defined later), and/or the ability of investors to implement system signals in actual market conditions. Such highly optimized systems are not designed to portray the worst-case scenarios but rather are developed to demonstrate optimum past performance. The belief that the future will be a carbon copy of the past is not only naïve, it is also a threat to your financial well-being.

WHY TEST A TRADING SYSTEM?

Is it necessary to test a system? After all, if testing a system can provide only hypothetical results with no guaranteed success in real-time trading, why bother testing? The answer is simple: Although it's true that you'll never really know with 100 percent certainty if a system will work in real time with real money, proper testing methods can allow you to learn the strong and weak aspects of your system. Following certain rules in developing and testing systems will increase the likelihood of their going forward effectively in real time. However, ignoring these rules or committing certain blunders will almost guarantee you that your system will not perform in the future no matter how good it looked in back-testing. Clearly, the emphasis must be on "proper" testing.

Traders have many reasons for testing systems. Some test a system just to go through the motions, failing to take the results seriously. All too often, they disregard the results or rationalize poor results. They mistakenly believe that they can turn a mediocre system into a winner by managing the trades differently or by practicing different money management rules. Other traders develop systems in order to market them to the public. Their objective is to optimize the system in order to reflect best-case performance. In effect, the ultimate product that they are trying to sell is a contrived system, curve-fitted to an extreme degree. This is the type of system that Roger (and thousands of other investors) purchased. As attractive as these products may seem, the odds of their making money in real-time trading are slim indeed because they were developed in order to show the best-case scenario. In effect they were retrofitted, or optimized, to show the best possible historical results. The systems are often highly complex with many factors and variables, each designed to make the past look good. Any statistician acquainted with the law of diminishing returns understands that the more variables and rules you add to the back-testing of a system, the less likely the system is to go forward with similar results.

The serious trader who tests systems with the rigor, realistic rules, and discipline needed for success in the markets must have specific goals. The reasons for testing systems are as follows:

1. *To determine whether a hypothetical construct is valid in historical testing.* How would the idea have performed in the past? This is not to be confused with being "fitted" to historical data.
2. *To learn the assets and the liabilities of the system.*
3. *To identify how potentially different timing indicators combine with one another to produce a potentially effective trading system.*
4. *To examine the relationship of risk and reward variables.* What are the variables (for example, entry and exit methods using stops, position, size, and the like) that would have produced the best overall performance with the smallest drawdown (to be explained more fully later)?

Since the time and expense of real-time testing a new trading system are considerable, it follows that computer testing is the most efficient method for determining how a system would have performed in the past. The main purpose of testing systems is to learn what might work best in the future based on what has worked in the past. Do not, however, expect to find a 100 percent correlation between the past and the future. Nothing is definite in the financial markets. Systems deteriorate, and rules are not 100 percent reliable.

There are various important aspects, which must be considered when you test any trading system. If and when you buy a system from any vendor, find out how the system was developed based on the following parameters.

Number of Years Analyzed

The further back in time you test a system, the more the results will represent reality. The sad fact is that many trading systems and indicators do not withstand the test of time. The further back you test, the less effective most systems will turn out to be. Many system developers prefer a standard test of ten years since it presents their systems in the best light. Be especially suspicious of systems that have been developed or tested on only a few years of data. They are unlikely to go forward in real time with similar results. Another important variable in testing systems is the number of trades used in the back-test.

Number of Trades Analyzed

Analyzing data over the course of many years is not necessary if you have a large sample size of trades. I feel that at least 100 trades are required to produce statistically significant results, provided your system will generate this number of trades in back-testing. It is better to err on the side of more rather than less data. Ideally, consistent results over 500 trades comprise an impressive test. It would not be wise to buy or use a system based on just a few trades that occurred during a circumscribed period of time. Such a system would not work in market conditions distinctly different than those tested.

Furthermore, it is possible to show impressive historical performance by using only a small number of trades. In having developed and back-tested literally hundreds of systems, we find that systems with high accuracy based on less than 50 trades in their sample tend to completely deteriorate when the same parameters are tested on 100 trades.

Here is an example of what I mean. Figures 12-1 through 12-6 show a series of back-tests using a simple moving average crossover system on Intel (INTC). As you can see from the notes on each chart, the number of trades in the sample and the length of time included in the study can make a marked difference.

Maximum Drawdown

A very important, but often overlooked, statistic is the percent equity drawdown. *Drawdown* is defined as the maximum amount of money a system has lost in consecutive losing trades. As an example, assume that I have $25,000 in my account. I make a trade that produces a $1000 profit. I now have $26,000 in my account. My next three trades are all winners for a total of $4000. My account is worth $30,000. I lose $1000 on my next

MovAvg (3) Crossover Intel Corp – NASDAQ-Daily 09/03/1998– 08/13/2001
Performance Summary: All Trades

Total net profit	$ 52641.00	Open position P/L	$ 453.00
Gross profit	$ 66287.00	Gross loss	$ –13646.00
Total # of trades	50	Percent profitable	68%
Number winning trades	34	Number losing trades	16
Largest winning trade	$ 16715.00	Largest losing trade	$ –5035.00
Average winning trade	$ 1949.62	Average losing trade	$ –852.88
Ratio avg win/avg loss	2.29	Avg trade (win & loss)	$ 1052.82
Max consec. winners	8	Max consec. losers	3
Avg # bars in winners	14	Avg # bars in losers	13
Max intra-day drawdown	$ –7784.50		
Profit factor	4.86	Max # contracts held	1
Account size required	$ 7784.50	Return on account	676%

Performance Summary: Long Trades

Total net profit	$ 27508.00	Open position P/L	$ 453.00
Gross profit	$ 32433.00	Gross loss	$ –4925.00
Total # of trades	25	Percent profitable	72%
Number winning trades	18	Number losing trades	7
Largest winning trade	$ 6902.50	Largest losing trade	$ –2566.50
Average winning trade	$ 1801.83	Average losing trade	$ –703.57
Ratio avg win/avg loss	2.56	Avg trade (win & loss)	$ 1100.32
Max consec. winners	4	Max consec. losers	2
Avg # bars in winners	13	Avg # bars in losers	12
Max intra-day drawdown	$ –4562.50		
Profit factor	6.59	Max # contracts held	1
Account size required	$ 4562.50	Return on account	603%

Performance Summary: Short Trades

Total net profit	$ 25133.00	Open position P/L	$ 0.00
Gross profit	$ 33854.00	Gross loss	$ –8721.00
Total # of trades	25	Percent profitable	64%
Number winning trades	16	Number losing trades	9
Largest winning trade	$ 16715.00	Largest losing trade	$ –5035.00
Average winning trade	$ 2115.88	Average losing trade	$ –969.00
Ratio avg win/avg loss	2.18	Avg trade (win & loss)	$ 1005.32
Max consec. winners	6	Max consec. losers	4
Avg # bars in winners	14	Avg # bars in losers	14
Max intra-day drawdown	$ –7527.00		
Profit factor	3.88	Max # contracts held	1
Account size required	$ 7527.00	Return on account	334%

Figure 12-1.   The 3-MA system in Intel, 1998–2001.

MovAvg (3) Crossover Intel Corp – NASDAQ-Daily 09/04/1990–08/13/2001
Performance Summary: All Trades

Total net profit	$ 45094.00	Open position P/L	$ 453.00
Gross profit	$ 81363.50	Gross loss	$ -36269.50
Total # of trades	230	Percent profitable	47%
Number winning trades	109	Number losing trades	121
Largest winning trade	$ 16715.00	Largest losing trade	$ -5035.00
Average winning trade	$ 746.45	Average losing trade	$ -299.75
Ratio avg win/avg loss	2.49	Avg trade (win & loss)	$ 196.06
Max consec. winners	8	Max consec. losers	14
Avg # bars in winners	11	Avg # bars in losers	12
Max intra-day drawdown	$ -9108.00		
Profit factor	2.24	Max # contracts held	1
Account size required	$ 9108.00	Return on account	495%

Performance Summary: Long Trades

Total net profit	$ 30176.00	Open position P/L	$ 453.00
Gross profit	$ 41875.50	Gross loss	$ -11699.50
Total # of trades	115	Percent profitable	52%
Number winning trades	60	Number losing trades	55
Largest winning trade	$ 6902.50	Largest losing trade	$ -2566.50
Average winning trade	$ 697.93	Average losing trade	$ -212.72
Ratio avg win/avg loss	3.28	Avg trade (win & loss)	$ 262.40
Max consec. winners	5	Max consec. losers	7
Avg # bars in winners	12	Avg # bars in losers	11
Max intra-day drawdown	$ -4562.50		
Profit factor	3.58	Max # contracts held	1
Account size required	$ 4562.50	Return on account	661%

Performance Summary: Short Trades

Total net profit	$ 14918.00	Open position P/L	$ 0.00
Gross profit	$ 39488.00	Gross loss	$ -24570.00
Total # of trades	115	Percent profitable	43%
Number winning trades	49	Number losing trades	66
Largest winning trade	$ 16715.00	Largest losing trade	$ -5035.00
Average winning trade	$ 805.88	Average losing trade	$ -372.27
Ratio avg win/avg loss	2.16	Avg trade (win & loss)	$ 129.72
Max consec. winners	6	Max consec. losers	7
Avg # bars in winners	11	Avg # bars in losers	13
Max intra-day drawdown	$ -13772.00		
Profit factor	1.61	Max # contracts held	1
Account size required	$ 13772.00	Return on account	108%

Figure 12-2. The 3-MA system in Intel, 1990–2001.

MovAvg (3) Crossover Intel Corp — NASDAQ-Daily 09/03/1980–08/13/2001
Performance Summary: All Trades

Total net profit	$ 38678.00	Open position P/L	$ 453.00
Gross profit	$ 81830.50	Gross loss	$ −43152.50
Total # of trades	426	Percent profitable	30%
Number winning trades	126	Number losing trades	300
Largest winning trade	$ 16715.00	Largest losing trade	$ −5035.00
Average winning trade	$ 649.45	Average losing trade	$ −143.84
Ratio avg win/avg loss	4.52	Avg trade (win & loss)	$ 90.79
Max consec. winners	8	Max consec. losers	57
Avg # bars in winners	13	Avg # bars in losers	12
Max intra-day drawdown	$ −15524.00		
Profit factor	1.90	Max # contracts held	1
Account size required	$ 15524.00	Return on account	249%

Performance Summary: Long Trades

Total net profit	$ 27128.00	Open position P/L	$ 453.00
Gross profit	$ 42204.50	Gross loss	$ −15076.50
Total # of trades	213	Percent profitable	33%
Number winning trades	70	Number losing trades	143
Largest winning trade	$ 6902.50	Largest losing trade	$ −2566.50
Average winning trade	$ 602.92	Average losing trade	$ −105.43
Ratio avg win/avg loss	5.72	Avg trade (win & loss)	$ 127.36
Max consec. winners	5	Max consec. losers	38
Avg # bars in winners	13	Avg # bars in losers	11
Max intra-day drawdown	$ −4562.50		
Profit factor	2.80	Max # contracts held	1
Account size required	$ 4562.50	Return on account	595%

Performance Summary: Short Trades

Total net profit	$ 11550.00	Open position P/L	$ 0.00
Gross profit	$ 39626.00	Gross loss	$ −28076.00
Total # of trades	213	Percent profitable	26%
Number winning trades	56	Number losing trades	157
Largest winning trade	$ 16715.00	Largest losing trade	$ −5035.00
Average winning trade	$ 707.61	Average losing trade	$ −178.83
Ratio avg win/avg loss	3.96	Avg trade (win & loss)	$ 54.23
Max consec. winners	6	Max consec. losers	28
Avg # bars in winners	12	Avg # bars in losers	13
Max intra-day drawdown	$ −17140.00		
Profit factor	1.41	Max # contracts held	1
Account size required	$ 17140.00	Return on account	67%

Figure 12-3.   The 3-MA system in Intel, 1980–2001.

MovAvg (3) Crossover Intel Corp – NASDAQ-Daily   09/05/1978– 08/13/2001
Performance Summary: All Trades

Total net profit	$ 37640.50	Open position P/L	$ 453.00
Gross profit	$ 81830.50	Gross loss	$ –44190.00
Total # of trades	455	Percent profitable	28%
Number winning trades	126	Number losing trades	329
Largest winning trade	$ 16715.00	Largest losing trade	$ –5035.00
Average winning trade	$ 649.45	Average losing trade	$ –134.32
Ratio avg win/avg loss	4.84	Avg trade (win & loss)	$ 82.73
Max consec. winners	8	Max consec. losers	57
Avg # bars in winners	13	Avg # bars in losers	13
Max intra-day drawdown	$ –6561.50		
Profit factor	1.85	Max # contracts held	1
Account size required	$ 16561.50	Return on account	227%

Performance Summary: Long Trades

Total net profit	$ 26709.00	Open position P/L	$ 453.00
Gross profit	$ 42204.50	Gross loss	$ –15495.50
Total # of trades	227	Percent profitable	31%
Number winning trades	70	Number losing trades	157
Largest winning trade	$ 6902.50	Largest losing trade	$ –2566.50
Average winning trade	$ 602.92	Average losing trade	$ –98.70
Ratio avg win/avg loss	6.11	Avg trade (win & loss)	$ 117.66
Max consec. winners	5	Max consec. losers	38
Avg # bars in winners	13	Avg # bars in losers	12
Max intra-day drawdown	$ –4562.50		
Profit factor	2.72	Max # contracts held	1
Account size required	$ 4562.50	Return on account	585%

Performance Summary: Short Trades

Total net profit	$ 10931.50	Open position P/L	$ 0.00
Gross profit	$ 39626.00	Gross loss	$ –28694.50
Total # of trades	228	Percent profitable	25%
Number winning trades	56	Number losing trades	172
Largest winning trade	$ 16715.00	Largest losing trade	$ –5035.00
Average winning trade	$ 707.61	Average losing trade	$ –166.83
Ratio avg win/avg loss	4.24	Avg trade (win & loss)	$ 47.95
Max consec. winners	6	Max consec. losers	39
Avg # bars in winners	12	Avg # bars in losers	14
Max intra-day drawdown	$ –17758.50		
Profit factor	1.38	Max # contracts held	1
Account size required	$ 17758.50	Return on account	62%

Figure 12-4. The 3-MA system in Intel, 1978–2001.

Performance Summary: All Trades

Total net profit	$ 45540.00	Open position P/L	$ −2008.00
Gross profit	$ 79457.50	Gross loss	$ −33917.50
Total # of trades	127	Percent profitable	65%
Number winning trades	82	Number losing trades	45
Largest winning trade	$ 10391.50	Largest losing trade	$ −3358.50
Average winning trade	$ 968.99	Average losing trade	$ −753.72
Ratio avg win/avg loss	1.29	Avg trade (win & loss)	$ 358.58
Max consec. winners	6	Max consec. losers	5
Avg # bars in winners	18	Avg # bars in losers	26
Max intra-day drawdown	$ −9123.50		
Profit factor	2.34	Max # contracts held	1
Account size required	$ 9123.50	Return on account	499%

Performance Summary: Long Trades

Total net profit	$ 25821.00	Open position P/L	$ 0.00
Gross profit	$ 40690.50	Gross loss	$ −14869.50
Total # of trades	64	Percent profitable	67%
Number winning trades	43	Number losing trades	21
Largest winning trade	$ 4360.00	Largest losing trade	$ −3358.50
Average winning trade	$ 946.29	Average losing trade	$ −708.07
Ratio avg win/avg loss	1.34	Avg trade (win & loss)	$ 403.45
Max consec. winners	5	Max consec. losers	3
Avg # bars in winners	17	Avg # bars in losers	24
Max intra-day drawdown	$ −8108.50		
Profit factor	2.74	Max # contracts held	1
Account size required	$ 8108.50	Return on account	318%

Performance Summary: Short Trades

Total net profit	$ 19719.00	Open position P/L	$ −2008.00
Gross profit	$ 38767.00	Gross loss	$ −19048.00
Total # of trades	63	Percent profitable	62%
Number winning trades	39	Number losing trades	24
Largest winning trade	$ 10391.50	Largest losing trade	$ −3171.00
Average winning trade	$ 994.03	Average losing trade	$ −793.67
Ratio avg win/avg loss	1.25	Avg trade (win & loss)	$ 313.00
Max consec. winners	5	Max consec. losers	3
Avg # bars in winners	20	Avg # bars in losers	28
Max intra-day drawdown	$ −6123.50		
Profit factor	2.04	Max # contracts held	1
Account size required	$ 6123.50	Return on account	322%

Figure 12-5.   A 3-MA system, 1990–2001.

Performance Summary: All Trades

Total net profit	$ 42379.00	Open position P/L	$ −2008.00
Gross profit	$ 102647.00	Gross loss	$ −60268.00
Total # of trades	229	Percent profitable	62%
Number winning trades	143	Number losing trades	86
Largest winning trade	$ 10391.50	Largest losing trade	$ −3358.50
Average winning trade	$ 717.81	Average losing trade	$ −700.79
Ratio avg win/avg loss	1.02	Avg trade (win & loss)	$ 185.06
Max consec. winners	8	Max consec. losers	5
Avg # bars in winners	19	Avg # bars in losers	28
Max intra-day drawdown	$ −12475.50		
Profit factor	1.70	Max # contracts held	1
Account size required	$ 12475.50	Return on account	340%

Performance Summary: Long Trades

Total net profit	$ 27787.50	Open position P/L	$ 0.00
Gross profit	$ 54146.50	Gross loss	$ −26359.00
Total # of trades	115	Percent profitable	68%
Number winning trades	78	Number losing trades	37
Largest winning trade	$ 4360.00	Largest losing trade	$ −3358.50
Average winning trade	$ 694.19	Average losing trade	$ −712.41
Ratio avg win/avg loss	0.97	Avg trade (win & loss)	$ 241.63
Max consec. winners	5	Max consec. losers	3
Avg # bars in winners	18	Avg # bars in losers	27
Max intra-day drawdown	$ −8108.50		
Profit factor	2.05	Max # contracts held	1
Account size required	$ 8108.50	Return on account	343%

Performance Summary: Short Trades

Total net profit	$ 14591.50	Open position P/L	$ −2008.00
Gross profit	$ 48500.50	Gross loss	$ −33909.00
Total # of trades	114	Percent profitable	57%
Number winning trades	65	Number losing trades	49
Largest winning trade	$ 10391.50	Largest losing trade	$ −3249.50
Average winning trade	$ 746.16	Average losing trade	$ −692.02
Ratio avg win/avg loss	1.08	Avg trade (win & loss)	$ 128.00
Max consec. winners	6	Max consec. losers	3
Avg # bars in winners	21	Avg # bars in losers	29
Max intra-day drawdown	$ −9091.00		
Profit factor	1.43	Max # contracts held	1
Account size required	$ 9091.00	Return on account	161%

Figure 12-6.   A 3-MA system, 1980–2001.

trade. My drawdown to date is $1000. I lose $500 on my next trade. My drawdown is $1500. I lose $2000 on my next trade. My drawdown is now $3500. As long as I continue to lose on successive trades, my drawdown continues to increase. If the next trade is profitable, then the string of losers is broken and the maximum drawdown to that point is $3500. Assume now that performance begins an upswing and soon a loss of $4500 occurs in a single trade. Since the $4500 is larger than the previous maximum drawdown of $3500, the new maximum drawdown is $4500. If the next trade loses $500, then the new maximum drawdown is $5000. This is how maximum drawdown is determined.

A system that generates a very high annualized percent return over a period of five years will be difficult to follow if it has drawdowns of 50 percent of account size several times during that five-year period. It would take guts on the part of an investor and a highly capitalized account to handle the equity swings. In my experience, a smooth equity curve is much more desirable even if it produces less overall profit. Theoretically, your account size must be at least twice the size of the maximum drawdown. Therefore, if you are considering a system that has $15,000 in maximum drawdown then you'd need a $30,000 account or larger if you're going to have a chance of being successful with the system.

This drawdown curve is important as it illustrates how practical your trading system will be with real money. It seems that most systems that offer the largest net profits have the largest drawdowns. Look at a large drawdown coupled with a string of losses, and it is easy to see why many people would prematurely abandon a potentially good trading system. People are generally more interested in trading systems that reflect steady growth and small drawdowns, rather than the home-runs showing large short-term gains with large drawdowns.

Maximum Successive Losses

While these can be painful, maximum consecutive losses can be useful. When you assess your losses, you will get an idea of how much emotional pain you may have to endure while trading your system. There are few traders who are willing to stick with their system after three or four consecutive losses. Oftentimes, they discard a potentially good system. Knowledge of this number can help prepare a trader for a worst-case scenario and prevent panic when it actually happens. If a system has shown ten losing trades in a row, then you ought to know about this vital statistic before you begin using the system. Some traders are not emotionally able to deal with that many consecutive losses without it adversely affecting their discipline.

Largest Single Losing Trade

This is especially important if it exceeds your normal risk control measure. There may be a problem or contingency you have overlooked. A natural tendency of traders is to overlook the learning opportunity presented by their biggest losing trades and to erase them from their minds.

If you pay attention to the largest single losing trade, you can learn where to adjust the initial stop-loss and manage the overall system with efficiency. You should also use this information to question why the largest single losing trade was bigger than the stop-loss you had selected. The whole idea of testing a system is to avoid surprises that can undermine either your performance or your psychology, or both.

Largest Single Winning Trade

In some ways it is more important to pay attention to the largest single winning trade since it can skew the net profit in an unreasonable way. It might be best to eliminate the largest winning trade in the system and then reevaluate the net results. As I mentioned earlier, the goal is to achieve consistency. An extremely large winning trade can misconstrue the overall results of the system's performance. If a system has shown $60,000 in net profits with $30,000 of the overall performance attributable to only one trade, then the average profit per trade goes down by 50 percent if the single largest winner is removed from the equation. This is a vital statistic. You want performance that is more evenly distributed across many trades.

Percentage of Winning Trades

This statistic is not nearly as important as you may think. It can often be highly misleading. For example, many successful traders and trading systems operate at 30 to 45 percent winners. Systems that reflect 80 percent accuracy can be bad systems if they lose more on the losing trades than they make on the winning trades. When you actually do some testing, you will see that it is difficult to achieve much over 55 percent winners in a system without falling victim to some serious limitations such as excessively large stop-losses or a large drawdown.

Slippage and Commission

Do not trust any testing results that do not include a reasonable allowance for slippage and commissions. Both can make a very big difference in your overall results. There are many trading systems that will make small steady profits when tested without slippage and commissions, then turn into steady losers when transaction costs are factored in. You must pay particular attention to the transaction costs when the system operates on short-term trades or day trading. The more often trades are generated, the more critical transaction costs become. Everyone has favorite numbers to factor in as transaction costs.

I like to use $15 for slippage and $20 for commission per round turn (a "round turn" equals 1 completed trade with commission in and out included) for a total of $35 per trade. This number may seem high, but I prefer to err on the conservative side and avoid unpleasant surprises. While you may initially want to exclude the transaction costs to simplify the operation, make sure they are included before you look at potential bottom-line results. Commission costs and slippage add up and can make an incredible difference in your testing results.

Ratio of Average Win to Average Loss

There is a tendency among traders to assume that you must have a proportionately high number of winners to losers in a system. Obviously, the ratio should be well over 1 to 1 (breakeven). Ideally we would all like to have a ratio of 3 to 1 or 4 to 1, winners to losers, but given a decent percentage of winners, a 2-to-1 ratio will produce plenty of profit.

Figures 12-7 through 12-10 illustrate the performance histories of several systems that we consider to be effective and correctly back-tested.

SUMMARY

Computer testing of mechanical trading systems has grown in the last ten years. The ability to verify claims of systems developers has increased due to the development of these testing systems. Today, however, systems developers use statistic manipulation to show optimum performance of a system. Oftentimes this is a distortion and does not adequately reflect how a system will perform in real time. The trader needs to be aware that systems developers massage statistics to market their trading programs. Learning to evaluate the validity of testing systems is just as important as the actual testing.

With so many traders using computers to design and test trading systems, it is important to examine the testing process itself and to identify the common mistakes that can affect your bottom line. It is important to remember that testing is the means to an end, not an end in itself and in realizing this you will become aware that reporting highly favorable results does not in any way guarantee success in the future. The goal of testing is to learn the good and the bad about your system and to begin to know what to expect in the future. A good trading system will reflect slow, steady growth and consistent performance.

Performance Summary: All Trades

Total net profit	$ 40832.50	Open position P/L	$ −2008.00
Gross profit	$ 18151.50	Gross loss	$ −77319.00
Total # of trades	330	Percent profitable	61%
Number winning trades	201	Number losing trades	129
Largest winning trade	$ 10391.50	Largest losing trade	$ −3358.50
Average winning trade	$ 587.82	Average losing trade	$ −599.37
Ratio avg win/avg loss	0.98	Avg trade (win & loss)	$ 123.73
Max consec. winners	8	Max consec. losers	5
Avg # bars in winners	19	Avg # bars in losers	30
Max intra-day drawdown	$ −12475.50		
Profit factor	1.53	Max # contracts held	1
Account size required	$ 12475.50	Return on account	327%

Performance Summary: Long Trades

Total net profit	$ 27615.50	Open position P/L	$ 0.00
Gross profit	$ 60008.00	Gross loss	$ −32392.50
Total # of trades	165	Percent profitable	64%
Number winning trades	106	Number losing trades	59
Largest winning trade	$ 4360.00	Largest losing trade	$ −3358.50
Average winning trade	$ 566.11	Average losing trade	$ −549.03
Ratio avg win/avg loss	1.03	Avg trade (win & loss)	$ 167.37
Max consec. winners	5	Max consec. losers	4
Avg # bars in winners	18	Avg # bars in losers	28
Max intra-day drawdown	$ −8108.50		
Profit factor	1.85	Max # contracts held	1
Account size required	$ 8108.50	Return on account	341%

Performance Summary: Short Trades

Total net profit	$ 13217.00	Open position P/L	$ −2008.00
Gross profit	$ 58143.50	Gross loss	$ −44926.50
Total # of trades	165	Percent profitable	58%
Number winning trades	95	Number losing trades	70
Largest winning trade	$ 10391.50	Largest losing trade	$ −3249.50
Average winning trade	$ 612.04	Average losing trade	$ −641.81
Ratio avg win/avg loss	0.95	Avg trade (win & loss)	$ 80.10
Max consec. winners	8	Max consec. losers	4
Avg # bars in winners	21	Avg # bars in losers	31
Max intra-day drawdown	$ −9178.00		
Profit factor	1.29	Max # contracts held	1
Account size required	$ 9178.00	Return on account	144%

Figure 12-7.   A 3-MA system, 1970–2001.

Performance Summary: All Trades

Total net profit	$ 77989.50	Open position P/L	$ −250.00
Gross profit	$ 188480.50	Gross loss	$- 110491.00
Total # of trades	575	Percent profitable	63%
Number winning trades	361	Number losing trades	214
Largest winning trade	$ 4360.00	Largest losing trade	$ −7234.00
Average winning trade	$ 522.11	Average losing trade	$ −516.31
Ratio avg win/avg loss	1.01	Avg trade (win & loss)	$ 135.63
Max consec. winners	9	Max consec. losers	7
Avg # bars in winners	10	Avg # bars in losers	19
Max intra-day drawdown	$ −11171.50		
Profit factor	1.71	Max # contracts held	1
Account size required	$ 11171.50	Return on account	698%

Performance Summary: Long Trades

Total net profit	$ 47330.50	Open position P/L	$ −250.00
Gross profit	$ 101777.00	Gross loss	$ −54446.50
Total # of trades	287	Percent profitable	66%
Number winning trades	188	Number losing trades	99
Largest winning trade	$ 4360.00	Largest losing trade	$ −7234.00
Average winning trade	$ 541.37	Average losing trade	$ −549.96
Ratio avg win/avg loss	0.98	Avg trade (win & loss)	$ 164.91
Max consec. winners	12	Max consec. losers	4
Avg # bars in winners	10	Avg # bars in losers	19
Max intra-day drawdown	$ −9812.50		
Profit factor	1.87	Max # contracts held	1
Account size required	$ 9812.50	Return on account	482%

Performance Summary: Short Trades

Total net profit	$ 30659.00	Open position P/L	$ 0.00
Gross profit	$ 86703.50	Gross loss	$ −56044.50
Total # of trades	288	Percent profitable	60%
Number winning trades	173	Number losing trades	115
Largest winning trade	$ 3047.50	Largest losing trade	$ −4921.00
Average winning trade	$ 501.18	Average losing trade	$ −487.34
Ratio avg win/avg loss	1.03	Avg trade (win & loss)	$ 106.45
Max consec. winners	8	Max consec. losers	6
Avg # bars in winners	10	Avg # bars in losers	19
Max intra-day drawdown	$ −7873.50		
Profit factor	1.55	Max # contracts held	1
Account size required	$ 7873.50	Return on account	389%

Figure 12-8.   A 3-MA system with different inputs, 1970–2001.

MovAvg (3) Crossover Lilly Eli & Co. – NYSE-Daily   09/20/1999–08/20/2000
Performance Summary: All Trades

Total net profit	$ 47196.50	Open position P/L	$ −1000.00
Gross profit	$ 75866.00	Gross loss	$ −28669.50
Total # of trades	58	Percent profitable	72%
Number winning trades	42	Number losing trades	16
Largest winning trade	$ 11393.50	Largest losing trade	$ −5528.50
Average winning trade	$ 1806.33	Average losing trade	$ −1791.84
Ratio avg win/avg loss	1.01	Avg trade (win & loss)	$ 813.73
Max consec. winners	16	Max consec. losers	2
Avg # bars in winners	5	Avg # bars in losers	12
Max intra-day drawdown	$ −8094.00		
Profit factor	2.65	Max # contracts held	5
Account size required	$ 8094.00	Return on account	583%

Performance Summary: Long Trades

Total net profit	$ 26606.00	Open position P/L	$ 0.00
Gross profit	$ 36684.50	Gross loss	$ −10078.50
Total # of trades	29	Percent profitable	83%
Number winning trades	24	Number losing trades	5
Largest winning trade	$ 8550.00	Largest losing trade	$ −5528.50
Average winning trade	$ 1528.52	Average losing trade	$ −2015.70
Ratio avg win/avg loss	0.76	Avg trade (win & loss)	$ 917.45
Max consec. winners	9	Max consec. losers	2
Avg # bars in winners	5	Avg # bars in losers	16
Max intra-day drawdown	$ −6609.50		
Profit factor	3.64	Max # contracts held	5
Account size required	$ 6609.50	Return on account	403%

Performance Summary: Short Trades

Total net profit	$ 20590.50	Open position P/L	$ −1000.00
Gross profit	$ 39181.50	Gross loss	$ −18591.00
Total # of trades	29	Percent profitable	62%
Number winning trades	18	Number losing trades	11
Largest winning trade	$ 11393.50	Largest losing trade	$ −3794.00
Average winning trade	$ 2176.75	Average losing trade	$ −1690.09
Ratio avg win/avg loss	1.29	Avg trade (win & loss)	$ 710.02
Max consec. winners	8	Max consec. losers	3
Avg # bars in winners	5	Avg # bars in losers	11
Max intra-day drawdown	$ −9237.50		
Profit factor	2.11	Max # contracts held	5
Account size required	$ 9237.50	Return on account	223%

Figure 12-9.   The 3-MA system in Eli Lilly, 1999–2001.

MovAvg (3) Crossover Lilly Eli & Co – NYSE-Daily   09/20/1990–08/20/2001

Performance Summary: All Trades

Total net profit	$ 67245.50	Open position P/L	$ –1000.00
Gross profit	$ 181696.00	Gross loss	$- 114450.50
Total # of trades	328	Percent profitable	63%
Number winning trades	205	Number losing trades	123
Largest winning trade	$ 11393.50	Largest losing trade	$ –5528.50
Average winning trade	$ 886.32	Average losing trade	$ –930.49
Ratio avg win/avg loss	0.95	Avg trade (win & loss)	$ 205.02
Max consec. winners	16	Max consec. losers	6
Avg # bars in winners	5	Avg # bars in losers	13
Max intra-day drawdown	$ –18170.50		
Profit factor	1.59	Max # contracts held	5
Account size required	$ 18170.50	Return on account	370%

Performance Summary: Long Trades

Total net profit	$ 48669.50	Open position P/L	$ 0.00
Gross profit	$ 91857.50	Gross loss	$ –43188.00
Total # of trades	164	Percent profitable	65%
Number winning trades	106	Number losing trades	58
Largest winning trade	$ 8550.00	Largest losing trade	$ –5528.50
Average winning trade	$ 866.58	Average losing trade	$ –744.62
Ratio avg win/avg loss	1.16	Avg trade (win & loss)	$ 296.77
Max consec. winners	9	Max consec. losers	4
Avg # bars in winners	5	Avg # bars in losers	12
Max intra-day drawdown	$ –9094.00		
Profit factor	2.13	Max # contracts held	5
Account size required	$ 9094.00	Return on account	535%

Performance Summary: Short Trades

Total net profit	$ 18576.00	Open position P/L	$ –1000.00
Gross profit	$ 89838.50	Gross loss	$ –71262.50
Total # of trades	164	Percent profitable	60%
Number winning trades	99	Number losing trades	65
Largest winning trade	$ 11393.50	Largest losing trade	$ –4262.50
Average winning trade	$ 907.46	Average losing trade	$ –1096.35
Ratio avg win/avg loss	0.83	Avg trade (win & loss)	$ 113.27
Max consec. winners	8	Max consec. losers	4
Avg # bars in winners	5	Avg # bars in losers	14
Max intra-day drawdown	$ –18519.50		
Profit factor	1.26	Max # contracts held	5
Account size required	$ 18519.50	Return on account	100%

Figure 12-10.   The 3-MA system in Eli Lilly, 1990–2001.

GLOSSARY OF TRADING TERMS

Amex   American Stock Exchange.

Analyst   An individual who utilizes fundamental and technical analysis to forecast a stock's price, company earnings, and so forth.

Ask   The price at which an individual, group, or firm is willing to sell stock.

Auction Market   A physical market, such as NYSE and Amex, where a specialist acts as an auctioneer coordinating buying and selling to investors making bids and offers in given stocks.

Back-Test   The process of evaluating the historical performance of a trading system, trading method, or indicator.

Bear Market   Market in which prices are generally declining.

Bid/Offer   A bid is an offer to buy at a given price, whereas an offer is an order to sell at a given price. Buyers bid for a given stock while sellers offer a given stock.

For example, if a stock is at 45 and you want to buy 100 shares at 43, you would place an order to buy 100 shares at 43 (100S@43), which would constitute a bid at 43. If you wanted to sell 100 shares at 47, this would be an offer at 47.

Breakout   When a stock's price moves past a previous support or resistance level.

Bull Market   Market in which prices are generally increasing.

Buy-and-Hold   Strategy involving the purchase of stocks for the longer term.

Correction   A less than 20 percent pullback in the market from its previous highs or a rally form its previous laws.

Covering a Short   When short sellers repurchase stock to replace the stock sold short.

Crossing of 75 percent and 25 percent   If one or both SI lines have been above 75 percent and one or both crosses below 75 percent on a closing basis for the given period, then sells can be considered. If one or both SI lines have been below 25 percent and if one or both crosses above 25 percent on a closing basis, then buys can be considered. Note that a more conservative variation of this application would be to require *both* SI lines to cross as opposed to requiring just one line to cross.

Curve Fitting   Curve fitting (or optimizing) is the act of fitting a trading system to past data. When a trading system developer optimizes a system, he or she does so in order to generate a set of system rules that have performed well on historical data.

Although the system appears to have worked well in the past, it is in fact "fitted" to the data. Hence, the system will frequently not perform well in the future. To a given extent, most system testing involves some degree of optimization or curve fitting.

Day Trade   A day trade is a trade that is entered and exited on the same day. It does not mean that the trade will be held overnight, that it will be kept overnight if profitable, that it will always be entered on the opening and exited on the close, or that it will not entail risk.

Day trades are always over by the end of the trading day. By definition they are no longer day trades if carried through to the next trading session. Day trades may be entered at any time during the day, but they must be closed out by the end of the day.

Day Trader   A person who day trades is called a day trader. A day trader is not an investor because day trades are not investments. A day trade is a speculation, and day traders are speculators.

Whether they do so in stocks, options, futures, mutual funds, currencies, or any other vehicle, a day trade is merely a speculative activity designed to capitalize on intra-day price swings.

Day Trading   Day trading is trading positions that are entered and exited on the same day.

Divergence with Price   If price makes a new high for a given time period but SI does not, then a top may be forming. If price makes a new low for a given period of time and SI does not, then a bottom may be forming.

Dollars per Share   How many dollars each share will cost you. When one says a stock is at 20, this is a short way of saying $20 per share.

Downtick   When the sale price of a stock is below its last price.

Drawdown   A decline in profits from a previous series of profitable trades.

FL   Floor Level or Initial Target.

Fundamental Analysis   An analysis process that looks at the fundamentals or basic issues of a company, for example, price to earnings (P/E) ratio, future earnings potential, dividends, income, debt management, market share, and a whole host of other aspects.

Fundamental analysis attempts to determine where a share price should be based on the company's current characteristics and future potential.

Fundamentalist   Someone who looks at a company's fundamentals to determine where the stock price should be.

Gap   When a stock's opening price is higher than the previous day's high or lower than the previous day's low.

Intermediate-Term Trading   An intermediate-term trade is one usually held for several months. Many traders, money managers, and investors prefer such trades.

Intermediate-term traders seek to take advantage of larger price swings but do not wish to hold stocks for several years or more. They seek to maximize their capital by holding stocks for larger moves over a period of months, thereby attempting to capitalize on large market swings.

Investing   A stock market investor can hold positions for several years or even for many decades. What the day trader does is the complete opposite of what the investor does but with one exception. They both try to make money, but they approach the task in distinctly different ways and with markedly different methods.

IT   Initial Profit Target.

Level I Data   The inside market quote—the highest bid and lowest ask price or what typical investors get when they call their brokers.

Level II Data   The full table of all buyers and sellers of a stock, showing who wants to trade, how many shares they are posting to trade, and at what price they want to trade.

Limit Order   When the purchaser of a stock sets a maximum price at which he or she is willing to buy, or the minimum price at which he or she is willing to sell.

Liquid   A stock that is easily tradable. A market that has sufficient trading activity.

Long   The purchase of a stock.

Long-Term Trading   A long-term trader may hold positions for several years, rolling contracts forward as they approach expiration. What the day trader does is the complete opposite of what the long-term trader does.

Lot   A lot is 100 shares of a stock. This is the normal minimum amount of shares bought or sold.

Margin   Money that your broker may let you borrow to allow you more trading power. Most personal stock trading accounts allow 50 percent margin, which means you can use two times the amount of your cash balance to buy and sell stocks.

Margin Call   Occurs when your balance falls below the minimum requirement for margin trading. When your broker issues a margin call on your account, you must sell (liquidate) some of your stock (to meet margin requirements) within a stated amount of time, or the brokerage firm does it for you.

Market Entry   Market entry means simply to establish a new long or short position. There are many different types of orders that may be used for entering and exiting markets.

Market Exit   Market exit means to close out an existing long or short position. Again, there are many different types of orders that may be used for entering and exiting markets.

Market Order   An order entered to buy at the current price.

Market Maker   One of the numerous participants who sets stock prices by balancing buy and sell orders.

Market Timing   A strategy that attempts to buy stocks at the bottom of a bear market and sell them at the top of a bull market. This strategy assumes that tops and bottoms can be easily picked.

MOM/MA   Momentum Moving Average.

Momentum   A combination of volume and volatility in a stock that keeps its price continuing in the same direction.

Nasdaq   National Association of Securities Dealers Automated Quotation System.

NYSE   New York Stock Exchange.

Odd Lot   Any amount of shares under 100. An odd lot may be anywhere from 1 share to 99 shares of stock. Buying and selling odd lots can be useful to the investor with limited resources.

Offer   A price at which someone is willing to sell a stock.

Optimization   The procedure used to create a trading system based on historical data is called optimizing (or curve fitted). A system developer optimizes a system in order to generate a set of system rules that have performed well on historical data.

 Although the system appears to have worked well in the past, it is, in fact, "fitted" to the data. The given system can be optimized several different ways and, depending on the method used, the results will have varying degrees of success in their ability to be replicated in the future.

Order Flow   The moment-to-moment incoming buy-and-sell orders received by specialists and market makers.

Oscillate   To move back and forth between extremes.

OTC   Over the counter—used with Nasdaq stocks.

Overbought   Stock prices are deemed to be too high to be sustained. If a stock is overbought, this could mean that a drop should follow.

Oversold   Stock prices are deemed too low to be sustained. The stock is oversold. This could mean that a rise should follow.

Overtrading   Trading too frequently.

Position   Holding shares in a certain stock.

Position Trader   As soon as a day trader holds a position overnight, he or she becomes a position trader. A position trader holds trades for an extended period ranging from months to years. The position trader can also be called an investor in stocks with a shorter time perspective.

Position Trading   When day trades are held overnight, they become position trades; therefore, when a trader holds his or her trades longer than a day (i.e., usually months to years) it is called position trading.

Price Chart   A graph on which the historical prices of a stock are plotted. Charts come in many forms, and help investors and traders gain a better perspective on recent and historical price movements. You can get charts for free at many financial Web sites.

Profit Taking   When a recent run-up in a stock's price brings sellers onto the market to take profits before the stock moves back down.

Quote   The highest bid and lowest ask price—the same as the *inside market.*

Rally   A run-up in a stock's price.

Resistance   The price level at which a market is expected to halt its upward trend and from which prices are expected to move lower at best, or sideways at worst.

Reversal   When a stock's price reaches a support or resistance level and turns around from there.

Round Turn   One completed trade, including commission in and out.

Scalping   The conservative practice of buying a stock, and holding it as long as a trend continues and then selling as soon as it appears that momentum is slowing.

In other words, ultra, short-term trading for very small but intra-day profits.

SEC   Securities and Exchange Commission.

Securities   Stocks or equities.

Sell-Off   A rapid decline in a stock's price.

Share   The basic unit of a stock. Shares are pieces of ownership in a company, which are bought and sold on a stock exchange according to the laws of supply and demand.

Short   To sell borrowed stock that you do not own in the hope of repurchasing it at a lower price and pocketing the difference.

Short Squeeze   When a stock that many investors have shorted goes up instead, causing the short sellers to have to buy to "cover their shorts," often causing the stock to rally further.

Short-Term Trader   A short-term trader is one who trades for relatively short-term market swings of two to ten days' duration. There is no firm definition of the exact length of time that short-term traders hold their positions.

Short-Term Trading   Short-term trading as opposed to day trading or position trading is trading for relatively short-term market swings of two to ten days' duration. Again, there is no firm definition of the exact length of time for short-term trading.

The distinction between short-term trading and position trading is not as precise as is the distinction between day trading and all other types of trading.

Slippage   Slippage is the tendency of a market to fall or rise very quickly, picking buy-and-sell stop orders very quickly. Hence, a $100 deduction for slippage means deducting $100 from every trade in a hypothetical back-test in order to represent more accurately what might have happened.

A market that tends to have too much slippage is, therefore, a market in which quick and sudden price moves tend to result in price fills, which are unexpectedly or unreasonably far away from your price orders.

SOES   Small Order Execution System.

Specialist   Acts as market maker in a given stock.

Spread   The difference between the inside bid and the inside ask.

Stochastic Indicator (SI)   A price-derived oscillator expressed in percentages. SI values approach 0 and 100 as limits. SI consists of two values, %K and %D. The SI period can be adjusted as desired. The shorter the period, the more the SI will fluctuate.

Stock Split   When a stock's price reaches a price level that appears expensive to the general public, a company will divide the price by a certain number of shares by the same amount.

Stop Order   A sell order typically placed just below where a stock's current price is to enable the seller to bail out of the stock if a price decline begins.

Support   The price level at which a market is expected to halt its declining trend and from which prices are expected to move higher at best or sideways at worst.

Tape   The listing for each stock that gives the time, volume, and price for each sale; same as the old "ticker tape."

Technical Analysis   Utilizes charts and graphs to determine where a particular stock's price is likely to be headed in the future.

Technician   Person who uses technical analysis to predict stock trends.

Timing Indicators or Timing Signals   A timing indicator is defined as any specific technique, whether fundamental or technical, which objectively indicates market entry, exit, or the underlying condition (i.e., bullish, bearish, neutral) of a given stock or market index. A timing indicator can also be called a timing signal as the terms are used interchangeably.

Total Share Cost   (Price per Share) × (Number of Shares) = Total Share Cost

Trading Range   The difference between the highest point and the lowest point of a stock move.

Trading Systems   A trading system is an organized methodology containing specific market entry and exit indicators, as well as an operational set of procedures (called rules) including, but not limited to, various risk management (follow-up stop-loss procedures) methods and procedures. A trading system is implemented by following specific timing signals that dictate market entry and exit.

Trading systems must be necessarily rigid in their construction for the purpose of delineating specific procedures which, theoretically, should lead to profitable trading, provided the system is functioning as intended or tested. A trading system must be systematic or it is not a trading system, regardless of what the individual who professes to be trading a "system" may think.

A few traders actually follow trading systems. The vast majority of traders begin with a system but alter it to suit their internal feelings about the markets to the extent that they are not following a system at all other than, perhaps, in their own minds.

Trading Technique   A trading technique is a fairly loose collection of procedures that assists traders in making decisions about market entry or exit. Frequently, a trading technique consists of one or more timing indicators combined with general entry and exit rules and/or risk management procedures.

A trading technique is, therefore, not a trading system but rather an approach to trading which is generally objective but not nearly as precise or rigid as is a trading system.

Trendline   A line drawn across either the price peaks of a stock trend or the price bottoms to emphasize the overall trend.

Uptick   When the sale price of a stock is higher than its last price.

Volatility   The rate and range at which variations occur in a stock's price.

INDEX

A

Abbott Labs, 34
Accumulation distribution, 72, 74–77
A/D oscillator (*see* Advance/Decline oscillator)
ADD method (*see* Advance/decline derivative method)
ADRs (American Depositary Receipts), 52
Advance/Decline (A/D) oscillator, 76, 78–81
Advance/decline derivative (ADD) method, 78, 80–81
ADX (*see* Average Directional Movement Indicator)
Agilent Technologies, 86
Alternative energy stocks, 122–123
Amazon.Com, 79–81
American Depositary Receipts (ADRs), 52
Analysis:
  fundamental, 175
  technical, 179
Analysts, 173
Antrim, Minna, 121
Ask price, 173
Auction market, 173

Average Directional Movement Indicator (ADX), 68, 70–71

B

Baby steps, taking, 149
Back-test, 173
Barteromo, Maria, 8
Batching, 173
Bayer, George, 67
Bear market, 72, 74, 173
Bid, 174
Bierce, Ambrose, 89
Biotechnology, 122
Bloomberg, 31
Boxes, 19–20
Breakout, 174
Brokerage firms, 38–41
Bull market, 72, 74, 174
Buy number, 68
Buy-and-hold, 174
Buying high/selling higher, 23–24
Buying low/selling high, 22–23
Byron, Henry James, 11

C

Chambers, John, 8
Channel surfing, 113–118

Charts (*see* Price charts)
Cheap stocks (*see* Low-priced stocks)
Checks and balances, developing a
    system of, 149
Chicago Tribune, 31
Chinadotcom Corp., 130–135
Cisco Systems, 8, 76, 77
CNBC.com, 31, 122
CNNFN, 31
Commission(s):
  on computerized trading systems,
    166–167
  costs, 39
  rates, 38
  trading, 6
Commodity Quote Graphics, 76
Computerized trading systems,
    153–172
  analysis of trades on, 158
  commission costs, 166–167
  maximum drawdown on, 158, 165
  maximum successive losses on,
    165
  need for caution with, 155–156
  percentage of winning trades on,
    166
  ratio of average win to average
    loss for, 167
  reality of, 154–155
  slippage, allowance for, 166
  and test of time, 158
  testing, 156–158, 165–167
Computers, using, 9
Control, 74
Corr Therapeutics, 83–84
Correction, 174
Cost, total share, 179
Covering a short, 174
Crossing of 75 and 25 percent, 179
Current indicators, 58
Curve fitting, 174

D

Darvas, Nicholas, 19–20
Datek, 31

Day trader, 174
Day trades, 4, 174
Day trading, 175
Day-trading system, essential
    elements of effective,
    82–83
DCA (*see* Dollar cost averaging)
Diary, keeping a, 146–147
Directional Movement Indicator
    (DMI), 68, 70
Discipline, 141–151
  and closing out the losers,
    145–147
  definition of, 142–143
  and fear, 147–149
  implementation as level of, 144
  individual nature of, 143
  and learnable skill, 149
  and luck, 143
  preparation/planning as levels of,
    144
  risk management as level of,
    144–145
  as "weakest link" in trading chain,
    143, 150
Discount brokers, 40–41
Divergence with price, 179
DJIA (*see* Dow Jones Industrial
    Average)
DMI (*see* Directional Movement
    Indicator)
Dollar cost averaging (DCA), 89–91,
    135–139
Dollars per share, 175
Dot coms, 2–3
Dow Jones Industrial Average
    (DJIA), 13, 91
Downtick, 175
Downtrends, 97
Drawdown, 158, 165, 175

E

Eli Lilly, 34
Elliott, R. N., 67
Entry, market, 176

E*TRADE, 31–32
Exit, market, 176

F

Facts, opinions vs., 7–8
Fear, 147–149
  of losses, 147–148
  overcoming, 149
  of profit, 148
The Financial Times, 31
Fitting the curve, 174
Five bar signals, 107–112
Franklin, Benjamin, 129
Frost, Robert, 27
Fuel Cell Corp., 123–125, 127
Full-service brokers, 40
Fundamental analysis, 175
Fundamentalists, 175

G

Gann, W. D., 67
Gap, 175
Gates, Bill, 153
Going public, 12
Greenspan, Alan, 8

H

Horace, 141
Horne, Richard Henry, 1
"Hot" stocks, 31–33
How I Danced My Way to Millions
  (Nicholas Darvas), 19

I

Implementation, plan, 144
Indicators, timing (*see* Timing
  indicators)
Information, 2
Initial public offerings (IPOs), 34–36
Insiders, 48
Institutional ownership, 47–48
Intermediate-term trading, 175
Investing, 4
  definition of, 175
  starting amount for, 5–7

Investment information services, 39
Investments, 4
IPOs (*see* Initial public offerings)

J

Japan, 18

K

Kennedy, John Fitzgerald, 55

L

Lagging indicators, 58–59
Lane, George, 65
Leading indicators, 57–58
Level I data, 175
Level II data, 175
Limit orders, 175
Liquid stock, 176
Liquidity, 44–45
Long purchase, 176
Long-term trading, 176
Losers, closing out, 145–147
Lots, 12, 176
  See also Odd lots
Low-priced stocks, 43–54
  buying and selling, 50–51
  and company characteristics, 45, 46
  with high short interest, 48–49
  and insider activity, 48
  and institutional ownership, 47–48
  mutual funds, 52–53
  and number of outstanding shares,
    46–47
  and outstanding shares, 46–47
  penny stocks, 51–52
  and "sex appeal," 49–50
  trading volume of, 44–45

M

MA indicators (*see* Moving average
  indicators)
MACs (*see* Moving average channels)
MAH (moving average of highs), 97
MAL (moving average of lows), 97
Margin, trading on, 7, 20–22, 176

Margin calls, 22, 176
Market entry, 176
Market exit, 176
Market gurus, 29–30
Market makers, 176
Market money, 28
Market orders, 176
Market timing, 176
Market(s):
    auction, 173
    bear, 72, 74, 173
    bull, 72, 74, 174
Maximum drawdown, 158, 165
Medical stocks, 34
Methods, trading, 57
Microsoft, 22
Momentum, 176
Momentum moving average
        (MOM/MA), 129–135, 139
"Most Actives" lists, 32
Moving average channels (MACs),
        95–119
    bar signals, 107–112
    buy and sell signals, 97, 100–107
    channel surfing, 113–118
    characteristics of, 95, 97
    daily, 96–99
    exiting positions, 107, 113
Moving average (MA) indicators,
        61–65
    and assets, 61–62
    and liabilities, 62
Moving average of highs (MAH), 97
Moving average of lows (MAL), 97
Multiple positions, 113
Mutual funds, 5
    dollar cost averaging with, 135–139
    low-priced, 52–53

N

Nasdaq, 13, 33–34
New York Stock Exchange (NYSE),
        32–34
The New York Times, 31
NYSE (see New York Stock Exchange)

O

Odd lots, 6, 12, 176
Offer (bid), 174
Offer price, 176
OHLC bar chart, 18
Online brokers, 38
Open-high-low-close (OHLC) bar
        chart, 18
Opinions, facts vs., 7–8
Optimization, 177
Order flow, 177
Order(s):
    limit, 175
    market, 176
    stop, 179
Oscillate, 177
Outstanding shares, 46-47
Overtrading, 177
Ownership, institutional, 47-48

P

Parabolic indicators, 68, 69
Patterns, looking for, 147
Penny stocks, 51–52
Pfizer, 34
Picking stocks, 27–36
    hot stocks, 31–33
    IPOs, 34–36
    medical stocks, 34
    tech stocks, 33–34
    and television investment guru,
        29–30
    and tips, 30–31
Planning and preparation, 144
Plug Power, 122
Popularity, 44
Position, 177
Position traders, 177
Position trading, 177
Price:
    divergence with, 179
    and timing, 59–60
Price charts, 13–18, 67–68, 177
Priceline.com, 49, 68, 126, 128
Profit taking, 177

Q

Qualitative judgments, 7–8
Quotes, 177

R

Rally, 49, 177
Rate of change (ROC), 72
Resistance, 60, 85–86, 93–95, 177
Reversal, 178
Risk capital, 5
Risk management, 144–145
ROC (rate of change), 72
Round turn, 178
RSI, 65–67
Rutherford, Ernest, 43
Rydex Biotechnology Fund,
    135–139

S

Scalping, 178
SEC (see Securities and Exchange
    Commission)
Securities, 178
Securities and Exchange
    Commission (SEC), 21, 47, 52,
    155
Self-discipline (see Discipline)
Sell number, 68
Sell-off, 178
Sex appeal, 49–50
Share cost, total, 179
Share(s), 11–12, 178
    dollars per, 175
    outstanding, 46–47
Short sell, 178
Short squeeze, 178
Short-covering rally, 49
Short-term traders, 178
Short-term trading, 178
SI (see Stochastic Indicator)
Signals, timing, 179
Slippage, 178
Specialist, 178
Split, stock, 179
Spread, 179

Squeeze, short, 179
Starting amounts, 5–7
Stochastic Indicator (SI), 65–67, 179
Stock spilt, 179
Stockbrokers, 37–42
Stock(s):
    choosing among (see Picking stocks)
    issuance of new, 12–13
    low-priced (see Low-priced stocks)
    penny, 51–52
    popularity of, 44
    shares of, 11–12
Stop losses, 107
Stop orders, 179
Support, 60, 83–85, 93–95, 179
Systems, trading (see Trading systems)

T

Tape, 179
Tech stocks, 33–34
Technical analysis, 179
Technicians, 179
Timing, market, 176
Timing indicators, 18, 56–82, 179
    accumulation distribution, 72,
        74–77
    advance/decline (A/D) oscillator,
        76, 78–81
    categories of, 57–59
    chart patterns/formations,
        67–68
    current indicators, 58
    directional movement indicators,
        68, 70–71
    importance of, 59–60
    lagging indicators, 58–59
    leading indicators, 57–58
    momentum, 72, 73
    moving average indicators (MAs),
        61–65
    parabolic indicators, 68, 69
    rate of change (ROC), 72
    stochastic indicators, 65–67
    usefulness of, 56
Timing signals, 179

Tips, trading on, 30–31
Total share cost, 179
Trades, 4
TradeStation, 76
Trading, 4
   day, 4, 174, 175
   intermediate-term, 175
   long-term, 176
   on margin, 7, 20–22
   over-, 177
   position, 177
   short-term, 178
   on tips, 30–31
Trading commissions, 6
Trading discipline (*see* Discipline)
Trading methods, 57
Trading range, 179
Trading systems, 56–57, 180
   See also Computerized trading
   systems
Trading technique, 180
Trading volume, 44–45
Trailing stop losses, 107
Trend-following indicators, 58
Trendline, 180
Trends, 60

TV analysts, 29–30
2chimps.com, 28

U
Upbid, 180
Uptick, 180
Uptrends, 97

V
Volatility, 180
Volume, 44–45

W
The Wall Street Journal, 31
Waters, James J., 76
"Whipsaw effect," 58–59, 68
Williams, Larry R., 76, 93
"Winners and Losers" lists, 32
Wordsworth, William, 37

Y
Yahoo!, 38

Z
Zeitgeist, 49

ABOUT THE AUTHORS

Jacob Bernstein is one of today's most popular and respected market analysts in futures and stocks. Bernstein is cofounder of the popular 2chimps.com stock market advisory Web site and the author of over 32 books on trading, including *Momentum Stock Selection* and *The Compleat Day Trader*. His research and trading methods are used by savvy traders all over the world.

Elliott Bernstein is cofounder of 2chimps.com, assistant market strategist, and a regular contributor to the Web site. His areas of expertise include technical analysis, timing, mutual fund investment strategies, stock sector analysis, and alternative energy stocks. He has been a guest on Internet business television and a contributor to the *Bernstein on Stocks* newsletter.